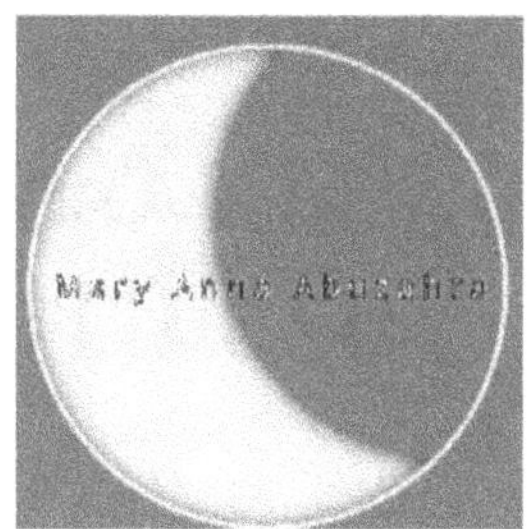

The Green Mountain Astrological Journal 2023: an astrological Moon, Earth & Sun journaling system

Plainfield, Vermont

Cover design: Mary Anna Abuzahra © 2023 – Background Night Sky image from Adobe Stock
Page design: Mary Anna Abuzahra, Green Mountain Intuitive Arts

Mary Anna is available for astrological consultations, astrological mentoring, presentations, lectures, and intuitive storytelling.

Contact the author through her website: maryannaabuzahra.com

A print version of this publication is available at most booksellers online or brick and mortar shops. The print version is Print on Demand. Please contact your local independent bookseller to help support your local economy.

The Green Mountain Astrological Journal 2023 UTC

Table of Contents

this page is purposefully blank

Why The Moon, Earth & Sun?

The repeating patterns of light and darkness of the moon's phases invite a personal reflection on our inner knowledge; helping us to experience a state of intuitive listening and alignment with the ever-changing cycle of nature. We can think of the moon phases as akin to the growth of plant life, from germination to flower to seed. The cycle of darkness and reflected light is imprinted within all life on Earth.

The moon cycle is due to the Moon, as well as the Sun and The Earth. Since we are ON the Earth, our viewpoint creates the imagery of the change in "moon phases" as the Moon orbits the Earth. Should we be viewing from another location, such as an astronaut would, it would all look different – especially eclipses!

And, of course, the Sun's light is on the surface of the Moon.
All three bodies – The Earth, Moon & Sun, participate in this pattern of light and darkness.
So, for more insight, I am including the Earth, Sun, and Moon together in this journal.

Using the Moon, Earth & Sun Journal

This unique Earth, Sun and Moon astrological journal includes Moon cycles, with astrological degrees of the Earth, Sun, and Moon at each of the eight common phases throughout 2023.
It also includes Sagittarius 2022 cycle to provide some transition. The Capricorn cycle which starts in 2022 and carries through to the start of 2023.

Astrological knowledge is not necessary, although helpful!
If you are new to astrology, you learn as you go, developing & deepening your knowledge through self-observation and journaling. If you have more advanced astrological skills, bring your resources and knowledge base to this focused work. The journaling entries that that you compose can also be aligned with tarot or oracle deck. Check my website for links to my Bookshop.org booklists. There, you find my recommendations for astrological books on signs and houses, and advanced astrological knowledge. When purchasing books, please support your local independent bookshop or order through my Booklist. Independent Booksellers to keep economic strength in our immediate communities.

The journal is calculated using the Tropical Zodiac and UTC (Coordinated Universal Time). You can use the journal as a basic astrological moon journal without your natal chart. For personalization of the journal, use your natal chart! It is important that your chart be calculated with accurate time of birth to make best use of this journal process.

Personalize your journaling by identifying the astrological degree of the Earth, Sun, and Moon each moon phase in your own natal astrological chart. Choose basic keywords for the natal house (noun) and the zodiac sign (adjective) to create a journal entry. This personalized journal sentence can be a starting point for further self-reflection.
Eclipses and Daily Ephemeris at Midnight UTC are included.

Should you need a copy of your natal chart: There are free opportunities to get your chart and natal moon phase online. You may also contact me through my website to order a digital file for a small fee.
It is not an automated process, so use the Contact form to reach me and send the Date. time, and location of birth. Please include how you would like your name to appear on your chart. I do not need street addresses unless you need a printed copy mailed directly to you. I will send you an invoice for the fee of $10 through PayPal, Venmo. Requests for printed and mailed charts are $20 to help with mailing costs. Your personal data is kept in strict confidence. Please specify your correct email address so that I can do my part to help keep your data confidential.

Astrological Consultations with Mary Anna: Discounts for Moon Journalers!
I am honored to collaborate with you! I offer a 20% discount for journaling clients! Please see my website for details and prices regarding astrological consultations. We will work together to identify your role and responsibilities in keeping our planet alive and abundant. You will discover how The Earth – our Gaia – is important in your chart, and what this unique and time-honored approach means at a personal and collective level.

Disclaimer, Guidelines & Directions

A note about journaling through this intuitive approach: sometimes staying constantly in tune with intuition and the empathic process can be overwhelming; a system of grounding and balance is required. Please find a grounding exercise that works for your individual needs. This journal process is not meant as a substitute for professional mental health or spiritual counseling, however journaling can often help as a supportive process to discuss with your professional service provider(s).

Guidelines:

- How do events in your own life align with the signs and houses in your chart as the Moon, Earth, and Sun transit through the whole cycle and through the entire year? Compose journal entries (sentences) to empower healthy choices in yourlife.
- For best accuracy in your daily life, convert each moon phase time & date for your time zone & Daylight Savings/Standard time in your own time zone. See page 144 for online links to several Time Conversion websites.
- Daily Ephemeris for the degrees of The Moon (at Midnight UTC) is posted for each moon cycle.
- Please contact the author should you need help getting up and running with your moon journal. I created this journaling process in 1997 as a tool to align with the moon's cycle of growth, development and decline, and the powerful archetypes of the zodiac with expressive and intuitive journaling. I have worked as a professional astrologer for over 25 years, working with individual clients, presenting workshops, lectures, research, and creating tools for deeper learning. The author has offered this monthly journaling process for groups and individuals since1997. This document is a copyrighted document. Please respect my efforts and suggest that friends purchase their own copies rather than copying the document to share. If you would like to attend or host your own Moon Journaling Circle – please reach out to me directly through my website for ideas, discounts and how you can best facilitate the Circle.

Directions:

<u>Step 1:</u> Check the Table of Contents for the page of the moon cycle for whichever cycle you are starting your journaling with. For best use, focus on the current cycle/phase that approaching at the time or that is current at the time. There are 9 pages per moon cycle. Locate the New Moon Journal Entry page. Update the time (and date if necessary) from UTC to your local time. It will be the same +/- until Daylight Savings changes it by one hour forward, the same when your local standard time changes backward. Note the zodiac degree for The Earth, Sun, and Moon. Check Natal Chart for these three degrees and write the Natal House number in the blank area under Moon, Earth & Sun. Become familiarized with the chart on the left side; you can learn to recognize the aspects/patterns between Earth, Sun, and Moon at each phase.

<u>Step 2:</u> On the <u>House Keywords column</u>, choose at least one key word for the Natal Houses that you identified in Step 1. (Circle your keyword/s) This keyword functions as a noun in your sentence composition. Choose words that resonate within you or relate to current trends in your life. Example for a Natal Chart where the degree may be in the 3rd House:

3rd House: my communications, my siblings, my neighborhood, short journey, journaling, writing, learning, curiosity, thinking

Step 3: On the New Moon journal entry page, note the Keywords for the zodiac sign and choose at least one keyword for the sign of the new moon. (Circle your keyword) This keyword will function as an adjective to the noun that you chose in your sentence building under new moon line. This sign and degree of the zodiac is the same for everyone, the House placement of the degree is your personal information. Choose words that resonate for you.

Step 4: On the journal entry page, clarify your sentence for the New Moon Phase.

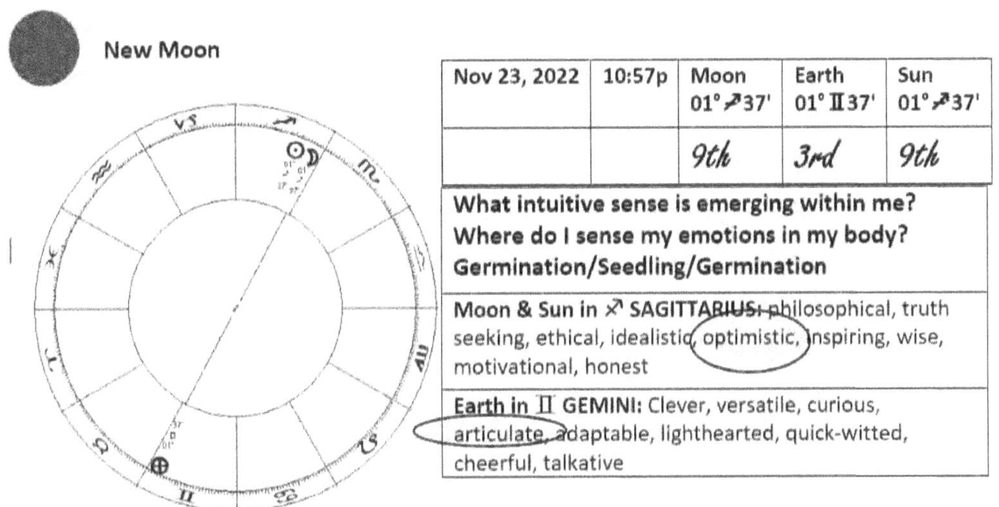

Nov 23, 2022	10:57p	Moon 01°♐37'	Earth 01°♊37'	Sun 01°♐37'
		9th	3rd	9th

What intuitive sense is emerging within me?
Where do I sense my emotions in my body?
Germination/Seedling/Germination

Moon & Sun in ♐ SAGITTARIUS: philosophical, truth seeking, ethical, idealistic, optimistic, inspiring, wise, motivational, honest

Earth in ♊ GEMINI: Clever, versatile, curious, articulate, adaptable, lighthearted, quick-witted, cheerful, talkative

I emerge with *optimistic and articulate exploration through journaling.*

STEP 5: Continue to journal your intuitive thoughts/experiences and choose a tarot card or other oracle or inspirational card or object and journal using your intuition of how these ties into your initial journal entry. Repeat these steps for each moon phase. Include the Sun's placement in your journaling process. Please note that the VERB for each phase is different, in alignment with the growth and decay of light of the entire cycle.

Crescent Phase is: **"I challenge myself to…."**

Please add in your own cultural, religious, and/or seasonal celebrations to your journaling.

Eclipses: dates and times are included and align with New and Full Moons. Eclipses can help with changes to bring in or move out things in our lives whether the eclipse is visible where we live or not. Please see the Table of Contents for eclipses. Check the entire year in advance to see when and what degrees the eclipses are in for Earth, Sun, and Moon – and what houses they are in your natal chart.

Importance of Your Natal Moon Phase & Natal Degree

- Your natal moon phase is an important key to understanding your natal chart. Knowledge of your natal moon phase can suggest a life-long approach or attitude that is helpful for you as well as others around you.

- Your natal moon phase is derived from theangle between the Earth, Sun, and Moon at the time of your birth. Use this online Moon Phase Calculator if you do not know your natal moon phase. Moon Phase Calculator: https://www.timeanddate.com/moon/phases/

- During each moon cycle, you can use your own natal recurring phase as a strong point during the cycle and schedule important activities or self-care during those few days. If you know the exact angle, you can pinpoint it each Month to the exact day and time, which is a creative period and has also been linked to conception/fertility.

- Your Natal Moon Zodiac Degree is also a key to understanding more about your chart and moon cycles. This degree repeats each moon phase and knowing the day each Month has also been linked to conception and fertility.

- If you are interested in learning more about your natal moon phase, phase returns and lunar degree returns, you can order a related consultation with the author or purchase a personalized list of these dates for the upcoming year.

Moon Phase Reference

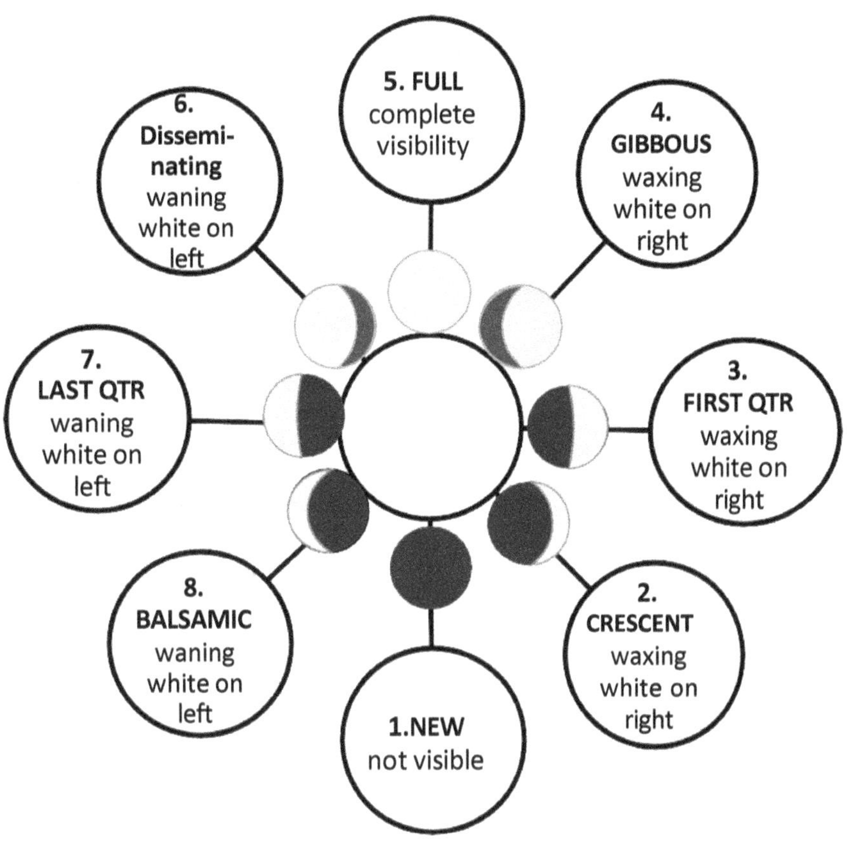

New: Emergence, Germination, 0-45° angle to Sun Winter Solstice/Moon & Sun conjoin/☽ ☌ ☉

Crescent: Struggle, Seedling, 45-90° angle to Sun: Semi-squares Sun, separating/☽ ∠ ☉ s

1st QTR: Action, Leaf/Stem/Root, 90-135° angle Sun Squares Sun, separating/☽ □ ☉ s

Gibbous: Structure, Bud, 135-180° angle to Sun Sesquiquadrate Sun, separating/☽ ⚼ ☉ S

Full: Fulfillment, Flower/Fruit, 180-225° angle to Sun Opposes Sun/☽ ☍ ☉

Disseminating: Share, Harvest, 225-270° angle to Sun Sesquiquadrate Sun approaching/ ☽ ⚼ ☉

Last QTR: Reorient, Decay, 270-315° angle to Sun: Square Sun, approaching/ ☽ □ ☉

Balsamic: Release/Resolve, Seed, 315-360° angle to Sun Semi-square Sun, approaching/☽ ∠ ☉

Astrological Reference

Signs & Correlations, abbreviations

♈ **ARIES**-assertive-1st House -Ar
♉ **TAURUS**-ownership-2nd House -Ta
♊ **GEMINI**-communication-3rd House-Ge
♋ **CANCER**-home-family-4th House-Cn
♌ **LEO**-selfexpression-5th House-Le
♍ **VIRGO**-routines-6th House-Vi
♎ **LIBRA**-partnerships-7th House-Li
♏ **SCORPIO**-deep sharing-8th House-Sc
♐ **SAGITTARIUS**-truthseeking-9thHouse-Sg
♑ **CAPRICORN**-authority-10th House-Cp
♒ **AQUARIUS**-friends & groups-11th House-Aq
♓ **PISCES**-immersion, prenatal-12th House-Pi

Planets

☉ **SUN**-identity
⊕ **EARTH** - commitment
☽ **MOON**-emotion
☿ **MERCURY**-communication
♀ **VENUS**-values
♂ **MARS**-action
♃ **JUPITER**-expansion
♄ **SATURN**-restriction
♅ **URANUS**-uniqueness
♆ **NEPTUNE**-creativity

Asteroids and Dwarf Planets

⚷ **CHIRON**-weakness into strength
⚴ **PALLAS ATHENA**-strategy
♇ **PLUTO**-transformation
⚶ **VESTA**-sacred focus
⚵ **JUNO**-partnering
⚳ **CERES** – nourishment

Modalities

CARDINAL: Aries/Cancer/Libra/Capricorn **FIXED:** Taurus/Leo/Scorpio/Aquarius
MUTABLE: Gemini/Virgo/Sagittarius/Pisces

More:

⊗ **PART OF FORTUNE** –physical connection to surroundings/environment
ASC **ASCENDENT**: presentation of self/mask (1st Hse Cusp) ("Rising Sign")
MC **MIDHEAVEN**: worldly impression of self/career (10th Hse Cusp)
DES **DESCENDENT**: partner/projection onto partner (7th Hse Cusp)
IC **INUM CEOLI**: family roots/ancestry (4th Hse Cusp)
NODES OF THE MOON: ☊ **North-**destiny ☋ **South-**past life skills

Keywords Houses and Signs

Adjectives	Nouns
♈ **ARIES:** assertive, courageous, independent, athletic, enthusiastic, aggressive, initiating	**1st House:** my body, my identity, myself, my appearance, my projected image, my soul-purpose, initial approach to life, my interests, my sense of me
♉ **TAURUS:** sensual, dependable, resourceful, deliberate, practical, comfortable, stubborn	**2nd House:** my talents, my resources, my physical possessions, my money, my personal self-esteem, my sensuous enjoyment, my self-worth
♊ **GEMINI:** Clever, versatile, curious, articulate, adaptable, lighthearted, quick- witted, cheerful	**3rd House:** my adaptability, my communications, my siblings, my neighborhood, short journey, my active search for knowledge, learning, curiosity, thinking
♋ **CANCER:** nurturing, attached, emotional, protective, psychic, domestic, intuitive	**4th House:** my home, family, heritage, my privacy, my emotional life, feelings, eating habits, receptivity, my protective urges, vulnerability
♌ **LEO:** self-confident, generous, playful, dramatic, courageous, brave, self-centered	**5th House:** my creative abilities, my self-expression pregnancy, children, pleasures, willpower, romance, merry-making, vacation, affection, confidence
♍ **VIRGO:** analytical, efficient, healing health-conscious, exacting, technical	**6th House:** my work conditions & habits, pets, my health, service offered, productivity, training, work skills, hygiene, clothing, nutrition & diet
♎ **LIBRA:** cooperative, fair, considerate, artistic, diplomatic, tactful, impartial, refined	**7th House:** agreements, contracts, partnerships, spouse, relationships, consultants, open enemies, receiving love, self-projection, social skills
♏ **SCORPIO:** transformative, sexual, secretive, musical, trustworthy, loyal, supportive, jealous	**8th House:** loyalty, partner's money & resources, taxes, inheritance, psychic & occult, transformation, shared values, sexual energy, investigations
♐ **SAGITTARIUS:** philosophical, ethical, idealistic, optimistic, inspiring, wise, honest	**9th House:** wisdom, justice, law, exploration, faith, religious & spiritual, higher education, foreign travel, legal action, experimentation, truth-seeking
♑**CAPRICORN**: disciplined, responsible, ambitious, professional, manifesting	**10th House:** accomplishments, authority, recognition, success, reputation, professional affairs, maturity, proficiency, honor, self-fulfillment, public image/life
♒**AQUARIUS:** humanitarian, innovative, progressive, eccentric, detached, friendly	**11th House:** groups & clubs, trends, friends, political awareness, emotional detachment, progressive thought, innovative technology & inventions, astrology
♓ **PISCES:** spiritual, subtle, empathic, psychic, vulnerable, intuitive, self- sacrificing, artistic	**12th House:** concern for others, self-sacrifice, psychological health, escapism, drug use, pre-natal imprinting, secret-keeping, surrender, spirituality

Questions, Outlook, Life Cycle

Listed below are open-ended questions, outlook And the corresponding plant life cycle.

New Moon: - Emerge: What intuitive sense is emerging within me? Where do I sense my emotions in my body? Germination/Seedling/Germination

Crescent Moon - Promise/struggle/Challenge: What is my challenge? What is my promise? Is my ego an asset or a liability? Sprout

First Quarter – Action: What steps will I take toward accomplishing my goals? How do I move forward? Root/Stem/Leaf -photosynthesis

Waxing Gibbous - Perfect and structure: How do I stay on track? What do I need to stay organized? What do I need to compromise? Buds appear and develop in size.

Full - Reflect and fulfill: How do function in my world with my process? What does it look like in my day-to-day world? Flower/Fruit

Disseminating/Waning Gibbous - Share: How can I share my experiences? How can I help others with my learning and experience? First harvest.

Last Qtr - Reorient My Perspective: How do I change- let go of patterns that do not serve my community? Decay/Last Harvest & composting.

Balsamic - Release, resolve, plan: How do I resolve this cycle, visualize, plan?
Seed is planted, and released to create the next cycle to germinate

♐ Sagittarius 2022

EPHEMERIS at MIDNIGHT UTC

Nov 23 2022	**17°Sc53'**
Nov 24 2022	**02°Sg15'**
Nov 25 2022	**16°Sg53'**
Nov 26 2022	**01°Cp39'**
Nov 27 2022	**16°Cp27'**
Nov 28 2022	**01°Aq08'**
Nov 29 2022	**15°Aq38'**
Nov 30 2022	**29°Aq51'**
Dec 1 2022	**13°Pi46'**
Dec 2 2022	**27°Pi22'**
Dec 3 2022	**10°Ar41'**
Dec 4 2022	**23°Ar45'**
Dec 5 2022	**06°Ta34'**
Dec 6 2022	**19°Ta12'**
Dec 7 2022	**01°Ge38'**
Dec 8 2022	**13°Ge55'**
Dec 9 2022	**26°Ge04'**
Dec 10 2022	**08°Cn05'**
Dec 11 2022	**20°Cn01'**
Dec 12 2022	**01°Le54'**
Dec 13 2022	**13°Le45'**
Dec 14 2022	**25°Le38'**
Dec 15 2022	**07°Vi37'**
Dec 16 2022	**19°Vi46'**
Dec 17 2022	**02°Li10'**
Dec 18 2022	**14°Li54'**
Dec 19 2022	**28°Li02'**
Dec 20 2022	**11°Sc37'**
Dec 21 2022	**25°Sc41'**
Dec 22 2022	**10°Sg11'**

1st House: my body, my identity, myself, my appearance, my projected image, my soul purpose, my initial approach to life, my interests, my sense of me
2nd House: my talents, my resources, my possessions, my money, my personal self-esteem, my sensuous enjoyment, my self-worth
3rd House: my adaptability, my communications, my siblings, my neighborhood, short journey, my active search for knowledge, learning, curiosity, thinking
4th House: my home, family, heritage, my privacy, my emotional life, feelings, eating habits, receptivity, my protective urges, vulnerability
5th House: my creative abilities, my self-expression pregnancy, children, pleasures, willpower, romance, merry-making vacation, affection, confidence
6th House: my work conditions & habits, pets, my health, service offered, productivity, training, work skills, hygiene, clothing, nutrition & diet
7th House: agreements, contracts, partnerships, spouse, relationships, consultants, open enemies, receiving love, self-projection, social skills
8th House: loyalty, partner's money & resources, taxes, inheritance, psychic & occult, transformation, shared values, sexual energy, investigations
9th House: wisdom, justice, law, exploration, faith, religious & spiritual, higher education, foreign travel, legal action, experimentation, truth-seeking
10th House: accomplishments, authority, recognition, success, reputation, professional affairs, maturity, proficiency, honor, self-fulfillment, public image/life
11th House: groups & clubs, trends, friends, political awareness, emotional detachment, progressive thought, innovative technology & inventions, astrology
12th House: concern for others, self-sacrifice, psychological health, escapism, drug use, pre-natal imprinting, secret-keeping, surrender, spirituality

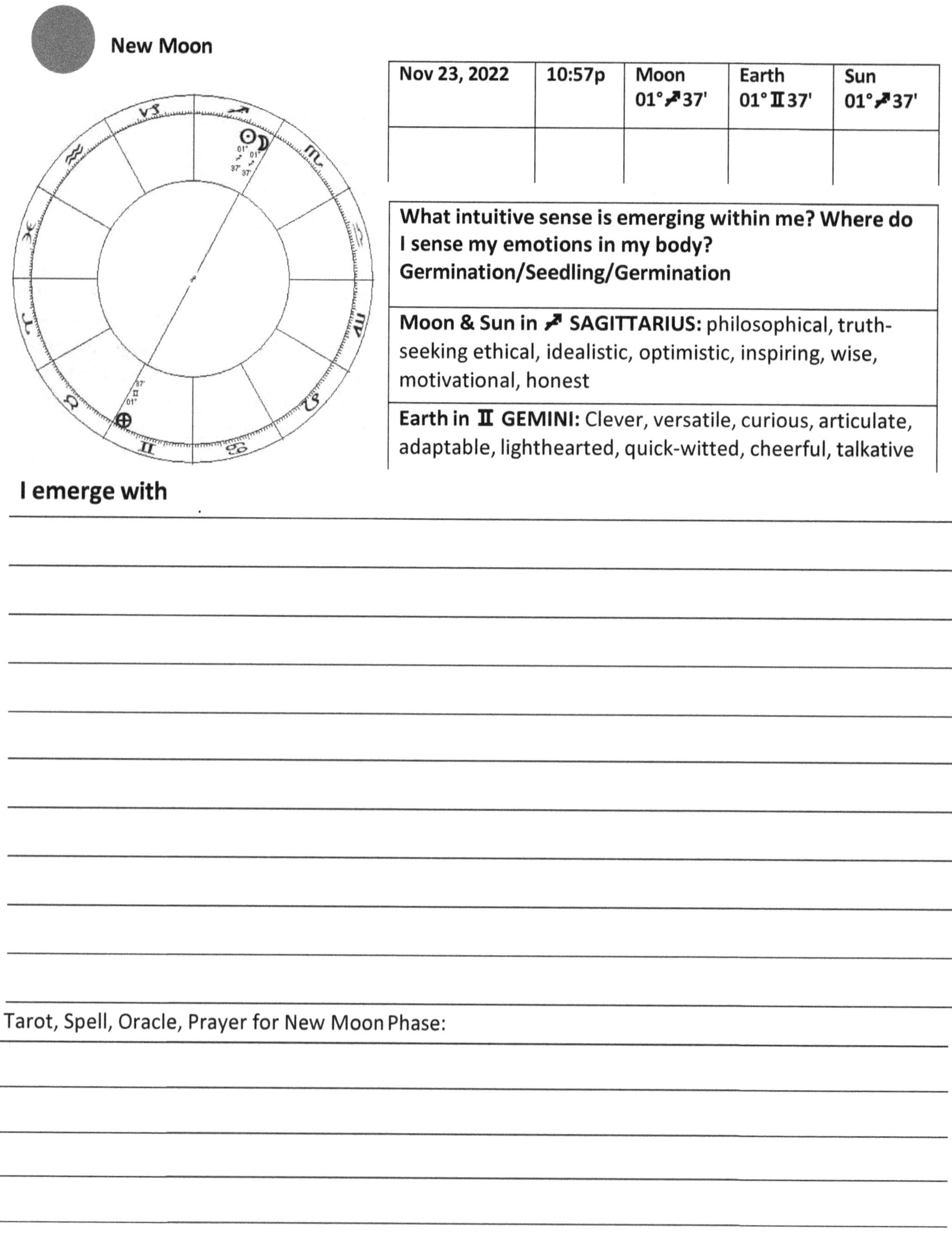

New Moon

Nov 23, 2022	10:57p	Moon 01°♐37'	Earth 01°♊37'	Sun 01°♐37'

What intuitive sense is emerging within me? Where do I sense my emotions in my body? Germination/Seedling/Germination

Moon & Sun in ♐ SAGITTARIUS: philosophical, truth-seeking ethical, idealistic, optimistic, inspiring, wise, motivational, honest

Earth in ♊ GEMINI: Clever, versatile, curious, articulate, adaptable, lighthearted, quick-witted, cheerful, talkative

I emerge with

Tarot, Spell, Oracle, Prayer for New Moon Phase:

Crescent

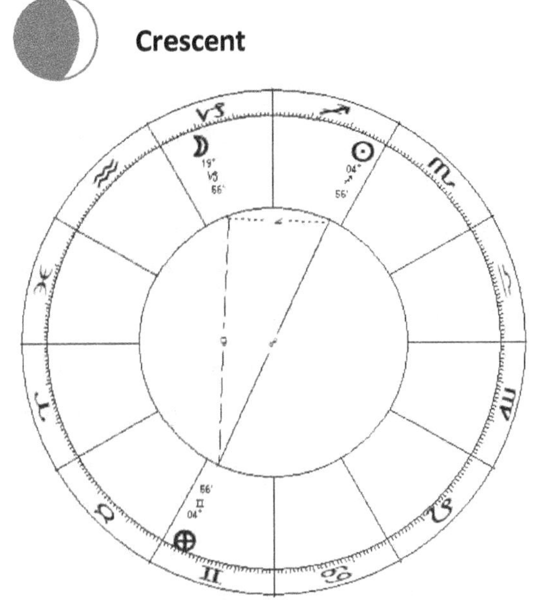

Nov 27, 2022	5:40a	Moon 19°♑56'	Earth 04°♊56'	Sun 04°♐56'

What is my challenge? What is my promise? Is my ego an asset or a liability? Sprout
Moon in ♑ CAPRICORN: authoritative, disciplined, responsible, ambitious, professional, manifesting
Earth in ♊ GEMINI: Clever, versatile, curious, articulate, adaptable, lighthearted, quick-witted, cheerful, talkative
Sun in ♐ SAGITTARIUS: philosophical, ethical, idealistic, optimistic, inspiring, wise, truth-seeking, honest

I challenge myself to ______________________________

Tarot, Spell, Oracle, Prayer for Crescent Phase:

First Quarter

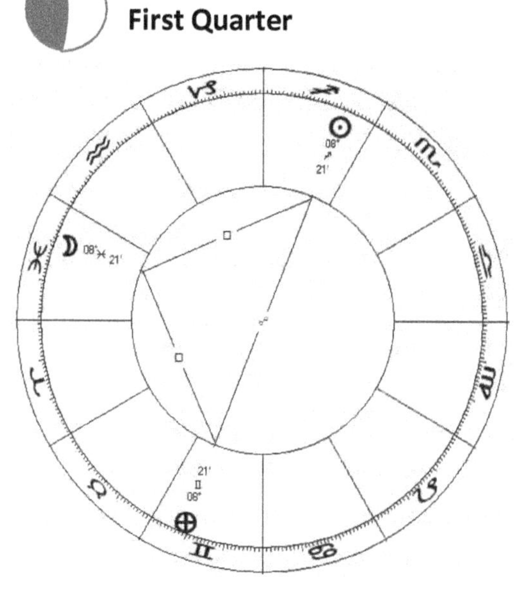

Nov 30 2022	2:36p	Moon 08°♓21'	Earth 08°♊21'	Sun 08°♐21'

What steps will I take toward accomplishing my goals? How do I move forward? Root/Stem/Leaf -photosynthesis
Moon in ♓ PISCES: spiritual, subtle, empathic, psychic, vulnerable, intuitive, self- sacrificing, artistic
Earth in ♊ GEMINI: Clever, versatile, curious, articulate, adaptable, lighthearted, quick-witted, cheerful, talkative
Sun in ♐ SAGITTARIUS: philosophical, ethical, idealistic, optimistic, inspiring, wise, truth-seeking, honest

I take action on

Tarot, Spell, Oracle, Prayer for the First Quarter Phase:

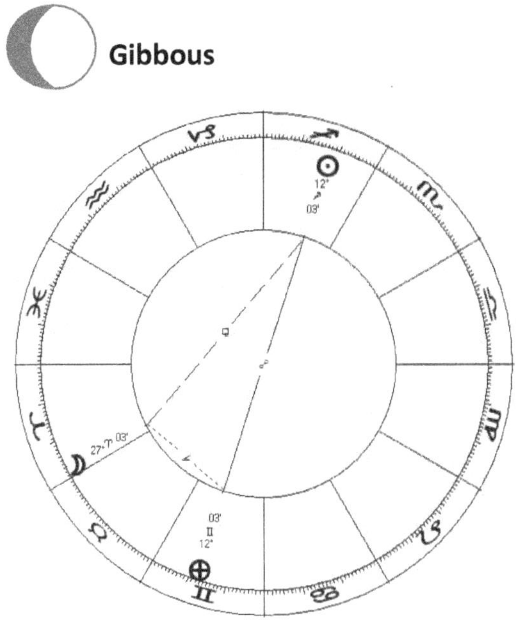

Dec 4 2022	6:08a	Moon 27°♈03'	Earth 12°♊03'	Sun 12°♐03'
How do I stay on track? What do I need to stay organized? What do I need to compromise? Buds appear and develop in size.				
Moon in ♈ ARIES: assertive, courageous, independent, enthusiastic, athletic, enthusiastic, aggressive, initiating, angry				
Earth in ♊ GEMINI: Clever, versatile, curious, articulate, adaptable, lighthearted, quick-witted, cheerful, talkative				
Sun in ♐ SAGITTARIUS: philosophical, ethical, idealistic, optimistic, inspiring, wise, truth-seeking, honest				

I develop structure with

Tarot, Spell, Oracle, Prayer for the Gibbous Phase

Full Moon

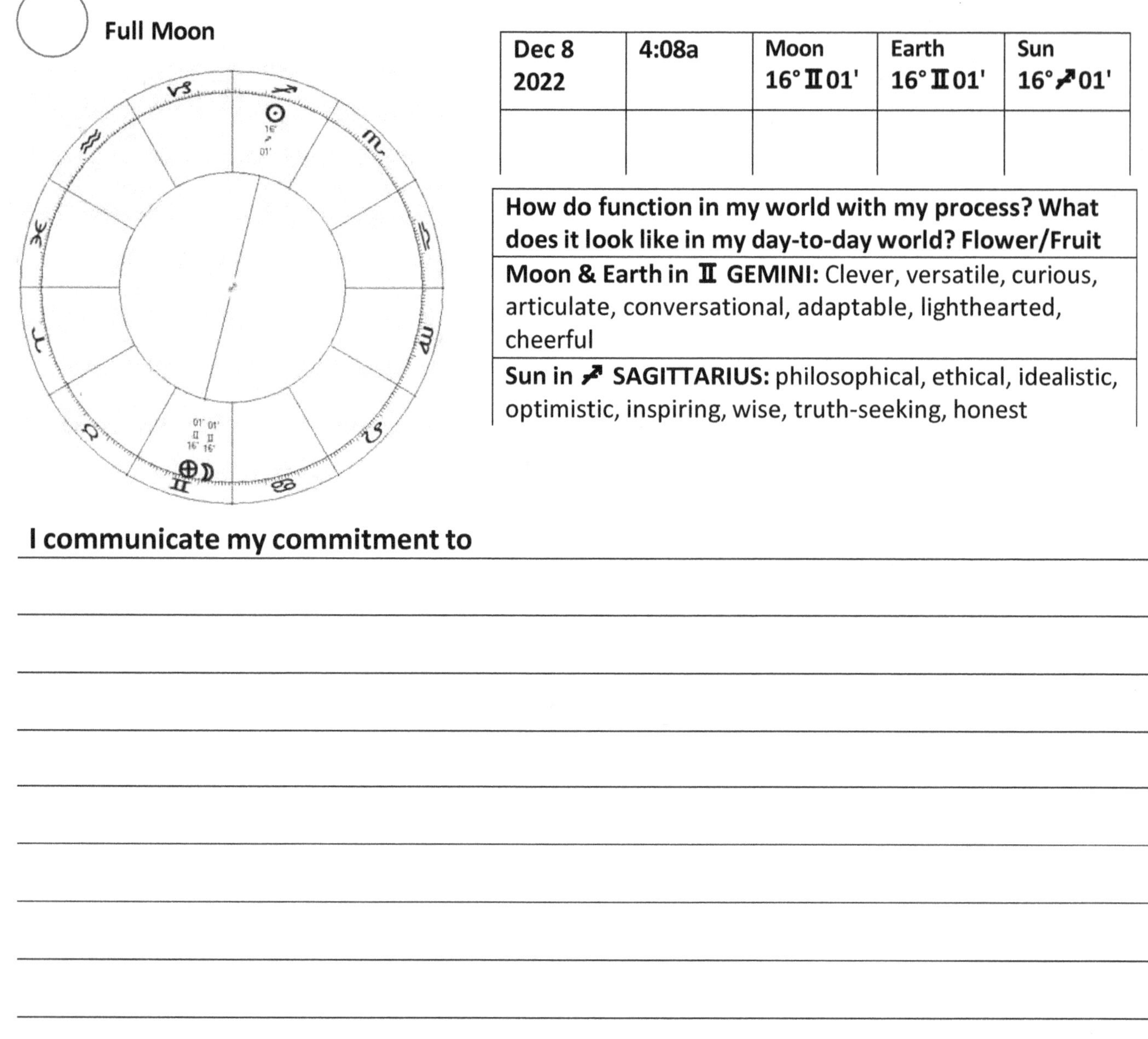

Dec 8 2022	4:08a	Moon 16°♊01'	Earth 16°♊01'	Sun 16°♐01'

How do function in my world with my process? What does it look like in my day-to-day world? Flower/Fruit
Moon & Earth in ♊ GEMINI: Clever, versatile, curious, articulate, conversational, adaptable, lighthearted, cheerful
Sun in ♐ SAGITTARIUS: philosophical, ethical, idealistic, optimistic, inspiring, wise, truth-seeking, honest

I communicate my commitment to

Tarot, Spell, Oracle, Prayer for Full Moon Phase:

Disseminating

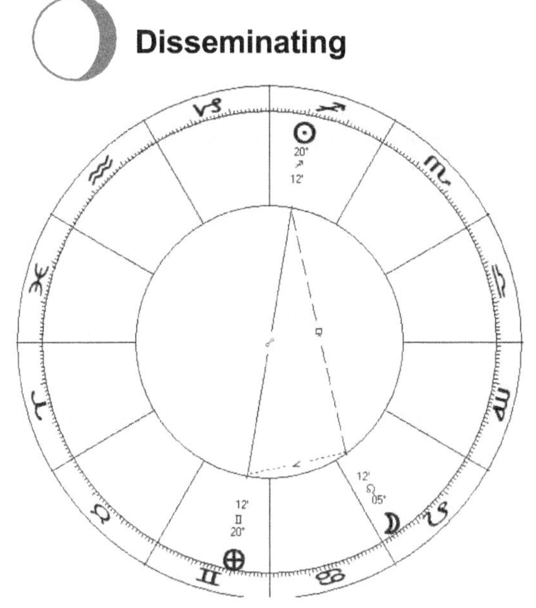

Dec 12 2022	6:40a	Moon 05°♌12'	Earth 20°♊12'	Sun 20°♐12'

How can I share my experiences? How can I help others with my learning and experience? First harvest.
Moon in ♌ LEO: self-confident, generous, playful, dramatic, courageous, caring, brave, self-centered
Earth in ♊ GEMINI: Clever, versatile, curious, articulate, adaptable, lighthearted, quick-witted, cheerful, talkative
Sun in ♐ SAGITTARIUS: philosophical, ethical, idealistic, optimistic, inspiring, wise, truth-seeking, honest

I share

Tarot, Spell, Oracle, Prayer for Disseminating Phase:

Last Quarter

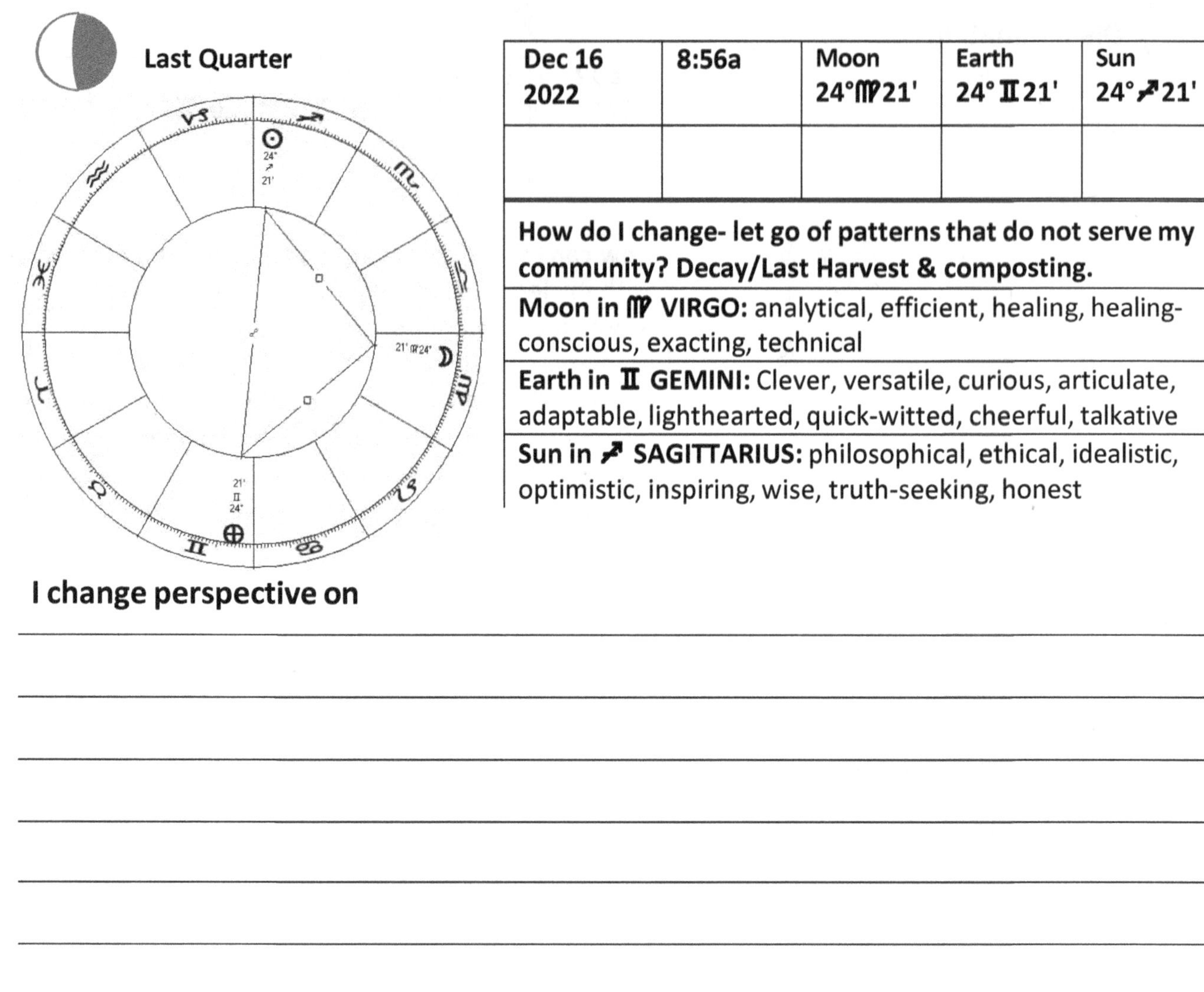

Dec 16 2022	8:56a	Moon 24°♍21'	Earth 24°♊21'	Sun 24°♐21'

How do I change- let go of patterns that do not serve my community? Decay/Last Harvest & composting.
Moon in ♍ VIRGO: analytical, efficient, healing, healing-conscious, exacting, technical
Earth in ♊ GEMINI: Clever, versatile, curious, articulate, adaptable, lighthearted, quick-witted, cheerful, talkative
Sun in ♐ SAGITTARIUS: philosophical, ethical, idealistic, optimistic, inspiring, wise, truth-seeking, honest

I change perspective on

Tarot, Spell, Oracle, Prayer for Last Quarter Phase:

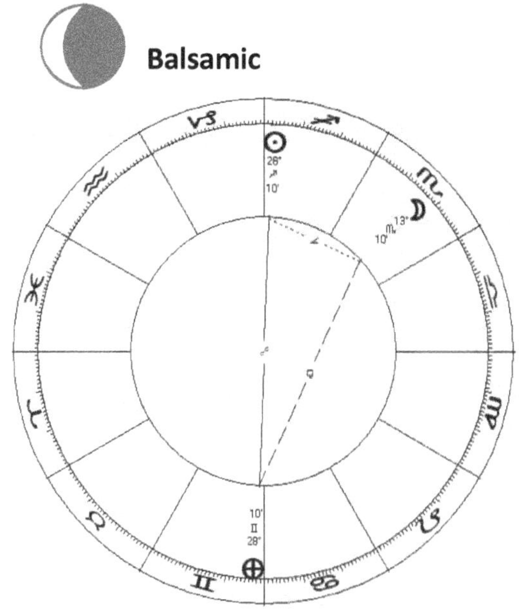

Dec 20 2022	2:40a	Moon 13°♏10'	Earth 28° ♊ 10'	Sun 28° ♐ 10'

How do I resolve this cycle, visualize, plan? Seed is planted, and released to create ate next cycle to germinate
Moon in ♏ SCORPIO: transformative, sexual, secretive, musical, trustworthy, loyal, supportive, jealous
Earth in ♊ GEMINI: Clever, versatile, curious, articulate, adaptable, lighthearted, cheerful
Sun in ♐ SAGITTARIUS: philosophical, ethical, idealistic, optimistic, inspiring, wise, truth-seeking,

I resolve/release and/or plan

Tarot, Spell, Oracle, Prayer for the Balsamic Phase:

♑ Capricorn 2022 -2023

EPHEMERIS at MIDNIGHT UTC	
Dec 23 2022	25°Sg05'
Dec 24 2022	10°Cp13'
Dec 25 2022	25°Cp25'
Dec 26 2022	10°Aq32'
Dec 27 2022	25°Aq23'
Dec 28 2022	09°Pi52'
Dec 29 2022	23°Pi55'
Dec 30 2022	07°Ar33'
Dec 31 2022	20°Ar46'
Jan 1 2023	03°Ta38'
Jan 2 2023	16°Ta14'
Jan 3 2023	28°Ta36'
Jan 4 2023	10°Ge48'
Jan 5 2023	22°Ge52'
Jan 6 2023	04°Cn51'
Jan 7 2023	16°Cn47'
Jan 8 2023	28°Cn40'
Jan 9 2023	10°Le33'
Jan 10 2023	22°Le25'
Jan 11 2023	04°Vi21'
Jan 12 2023	16°Vi21'
Jan 13 2023	28°Vi29'
Jan 14 2023	10°Li50'
Jan 15 2023	23°Li28'
Jan 16 2023	06°Sc28'
Jan 17 2023	19°Sc53'
Jan 18 2023	03°Sg47'
Jan 19 2023	18°Sg10'
Jan 20 2023	03°Cp00'

1st House: my body, my identity, myself, my appearance, my projected image, my soul purpose, my initial approach to life, my interests, my sense of me
2nd House: my talents, my resources, my possessions, my money, my personal self-esteem, my sensuous enjoyment, my self-worth
3rd House: my adaptability, my communications, my siblings, my neighborhood, short journey, my active search for knowledge, learning, curiosity, thinking
4th House: my home, family, heritage, my privacy, my emotional life, feelings, eating habits, receptivity, my protective urges, vulnerability
5th House: my creative abilities, my self-expression pregnancy, children, pleasures, willpower, romance, merry-making vacation, affection, confidence
6th House: my work conditions & habits, pets, my health, service offered, productivity, training, work skills, hygiene, clothing, nutrition & diet
7th House: agreements, contracts, partnerships, spouse, relationships, consultants, open enemies, receiving love, self-projection, social skills
8th House: loyalty, partner's money & resources, taxes, inheritance, psychic & occult, transformation, shared values, sexual energy, investigations
9th House: wisdom, justice, law, exploration, faith, religious & spiritual, higher education, foreign travel, legal action, experimentation, truth-seeking
10th House: accomplishments, authority, recognition, success, reputation, professional affairs, maturity, proficiency, honor, self-fulfillment, public image/life
11th House: groups & clubs, trends, friends, political awareness, emotional detachment, progressive thought, innovative technology & inventions, astrology
12th House: concern for others, self-sacrifice, psychological health, escapism, drug use, pre-natal imprinting, secret-keeping, surrender, spirituality

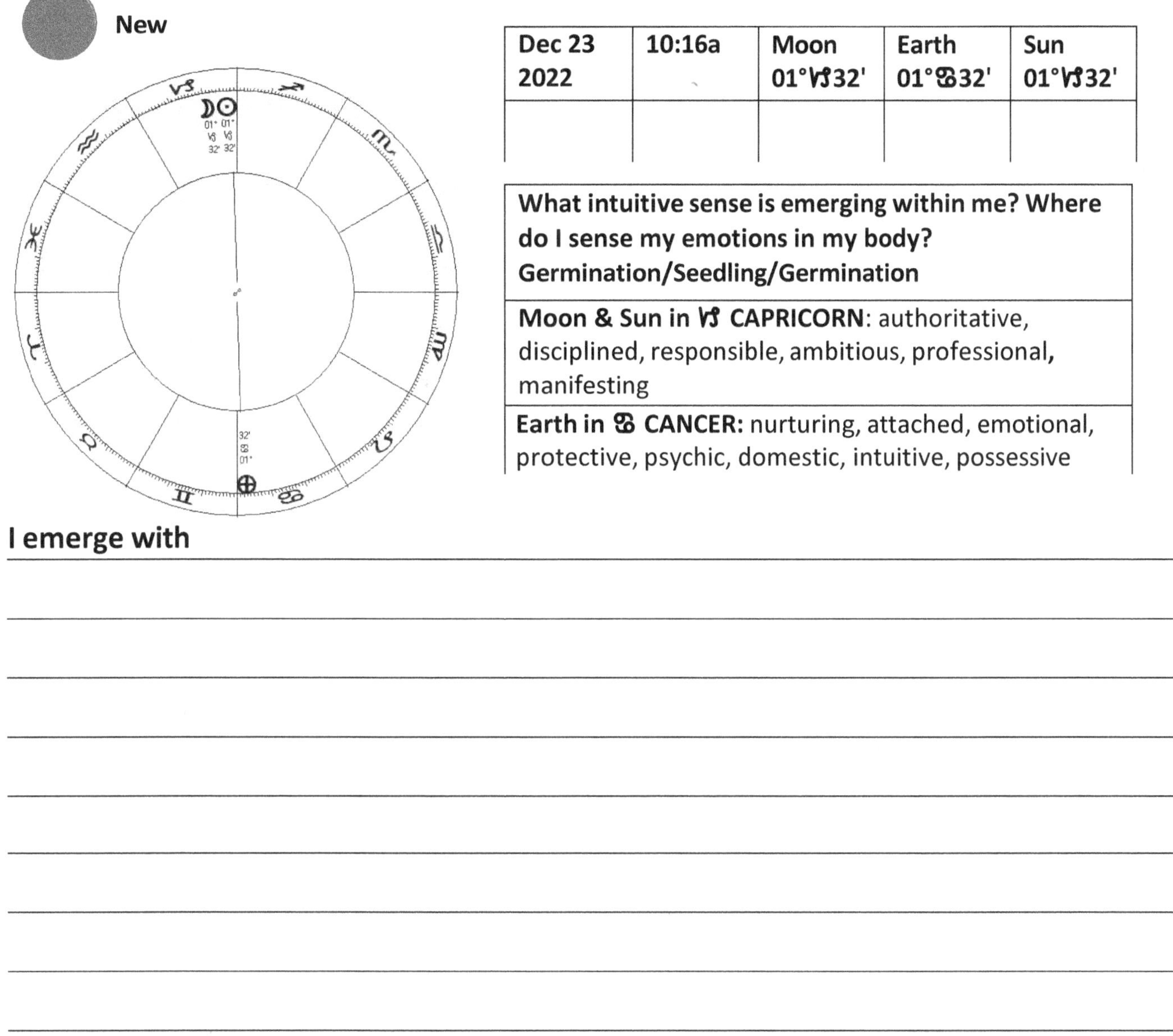

New

Dec 23 2022	10:16a	Moon 01°♑32'	Earth 01°♋32'	Sun 01°♑32'

What intuitive sense is emerging within me? Where do I sense my emotions in my body? Germination/Seedling/Germination

Moon & Sun in ♑ CAPRICORN: authoritative, disciplined, responsible, ambitious, professional**,** manifesting

Earth in ♋ CANCER: nurturing, attached, emotional, protective, psychic, domestic, intuitive, possessive

I emerge with

Tarot, Spell, Oracle, Prayer for New Moon Phase

Crescent

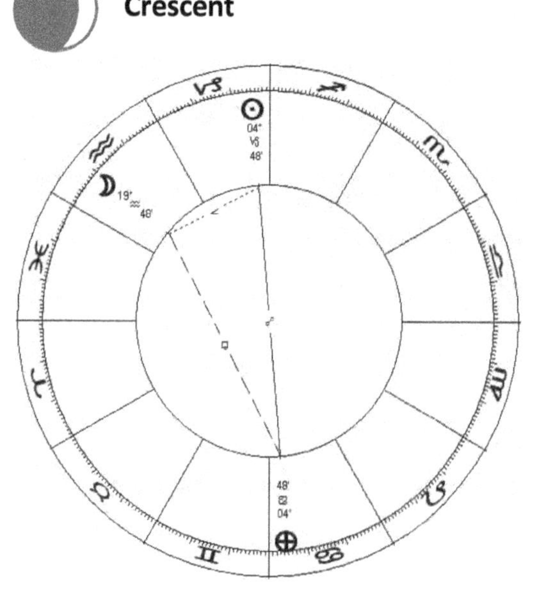

Dec 26 2022	2:54p	Moon 19°♒48'	Earth 04°♋48'	Sun 04°♑48'

What is my challenge? What is my promise? Is my ego an asset or a liability? Sprout
Moon in ♒AQUARIUS: humanitarian, innovative, progressive, eccentric, detached, friendly, generous
Earth in ♋ CANCER: nurturing, attached, emotional, protective, psychic, domestic, intuitive, possessive
Sun in ♑ CAPRICORN: authoritative, disciplined, responsible, ambitious, professional, manifesting

I challenge myself to

Tarot, Spell, Oracle, Prayer for Crescent Phase:

First Quarter

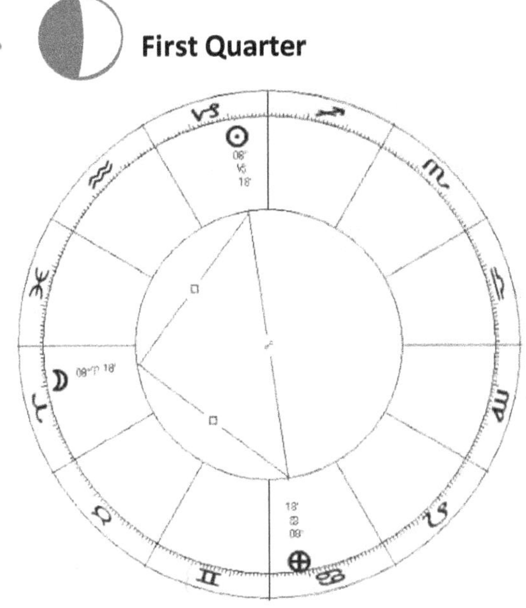

Dec 30, 2022	1:20a	Moon 08°♈18'	Earth 08°♋18'	Sun 08°♑18'

What steps will I take toward accomplishing my goals? How do I move forward? Root/Stem/Leaf - photosynthesis
Moon in ♈ ARIES: assertive, courageous, independent, enthusiastic, athletic, enthusiastic, active, aggressive, initiating, focused, forward, direct
Earth in ♋ CANCER: nurturing, attached, emotional, protective, psychic, domestic, intuitive
Sun in ♑ CAPRICORN: disciplined, responsible, practical, successful, ambitious, professional, manifesting

I take action on

Tarot, Spell, Oracle, Prayer for First Quarter Phase:

Gibbous

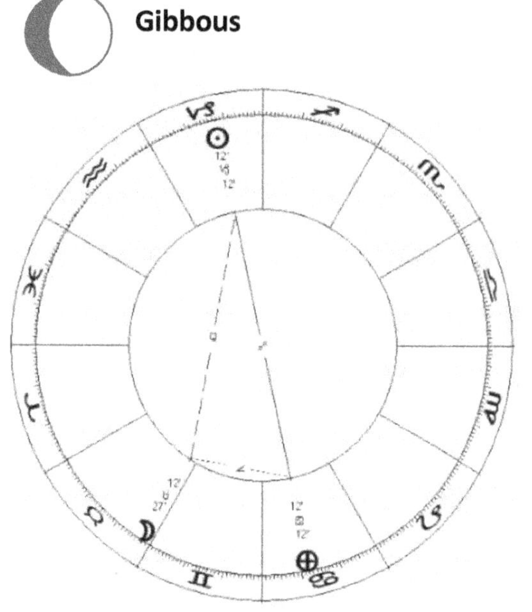

Jan 2 2023	9:16p	Moon 27° ♉ 12'	Earth 12° ♋ 12'	Sun 12° ♑ 12'

How do I stay on track? What do I need to stay organized? What do I need to compromise? Buds appear and develop in size.
Moon in ♉ Taurus: sensual, dependable, resourceful, deliberate, practical, comfortable, stubborn
Earth in ♋ Cancer: nurturing, attached, psychic, emotional, protective, domestic, intuitive
Sun in ♑ CAPRICORN: authoritative, disciplined, responsible, practical, successful, ambitious, professional, manifesting

I develop structure with

Tarot, Spell, Oracle, Prayer for Gibbous Phase:

Full

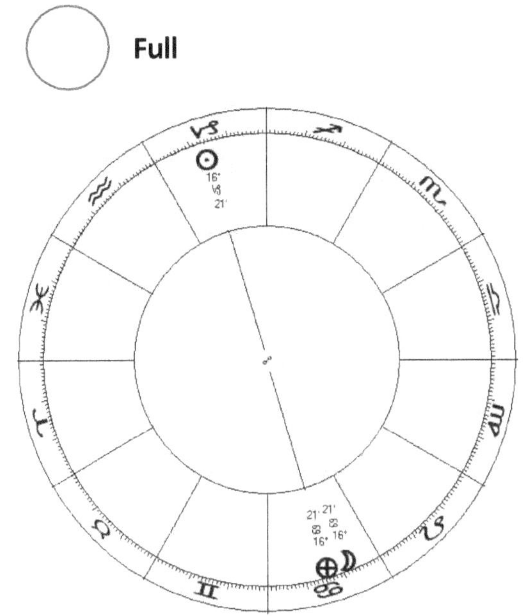

Jan 6 2023	11:07p	Moon 16°♋21'	Earth 16°♋21'	Sun 16°♑21'

How do function in my world with my process? What does it look like in my day-to-day world? Flower/Fruit
Moon & Earth in ♋ CANCER: nurturing, attached, emotional, protective, psychic, domestic, intuitive
Sun in ♑ CAPRICORN: disciplined, responsible, ambitious, professional, manifesting

I communicate my commitment to

Tarot, Spell, Oracle, Prayer for Full Moon Phase:

Disseminating

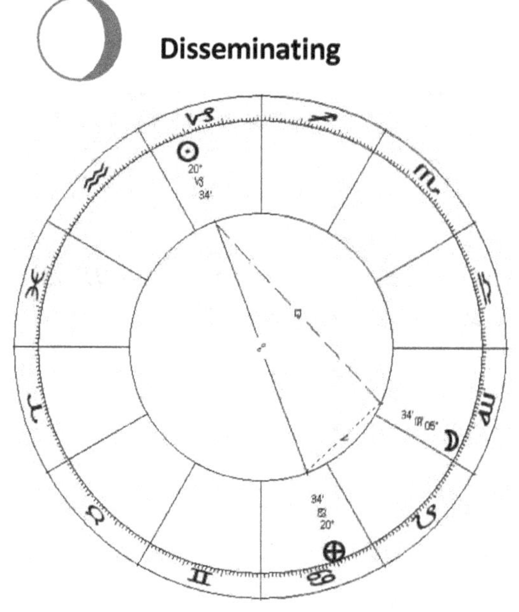

Jan 11 2023	2:27a	Moon 05°♍34'	Earth 20°♋34'	Sun 20°♑34'

How can I share my experiences? How can I help others with my learning and experience? First harvest.
Moon in ♍ VIRGO: analytical, efficient, healing health-conscious, exacting, technical
Earth in ♋ CANCER: nurturing, attached, emotional, protective, psychic, domestic, intuitive
Sun in ♑ CAPRICORN: disciplined, responsible, ambitious, professional, manifesting

I share

Tarot, Spell, Oracle, Prayer for Disseminating Phase:

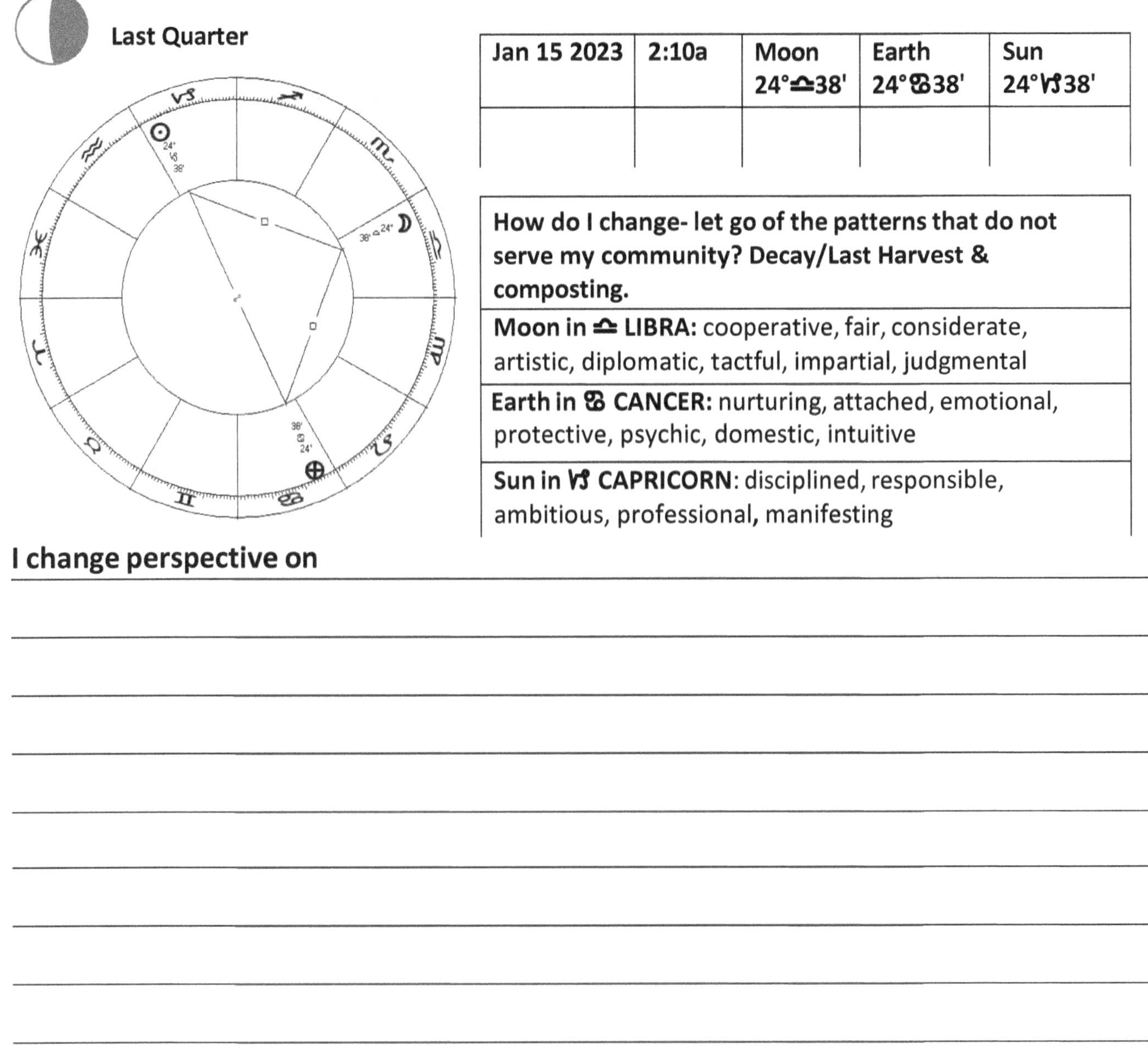

Last Quarter

Jan 15 2023	2:10a	Moon 24°♎38'	Earth 24°♋38'	Sun 24°♑38'

How do I change- let go of the patterns that do not serve my community? Decay/Last Harvest & composting.
Moon in ♎ LIBRA: cooperative, fair, considerate, artistic, diplomatic, tactful, impartial, judgmental
Earth in ♋ CANCER: nurturing, attached, emotional, protective, psychic, domestic, intuitive
Sun in ♑ CAPRICORN: disciplined, responsible, ambitious, professional, manifesting

I change perspective on

Tarot, Spell, Oracle, Prayer for Last QuarterPhase:

Balsamic

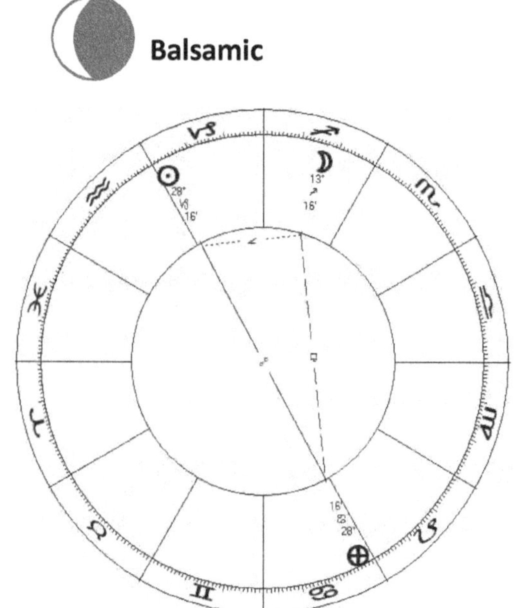

Jan 18 2023	3:55p	Moon 13°♐16'	Earth 28°♋16'	Sun 28°♑16'

How do I resolve this cycle & visualize, plan? Seed is planted, released to create next cycle/ germination begins.
Moon in ♐ SAGITTARIUS: expansive, philosophical, ethical, idealistic, optimistic, inspiring, wise, truth-seeking, honest
Earth in ♋ CANCER: nurturing, attached, emotional, protective, psychic, domestic, intuitive
Sun in ♑ CAPRICORN: disciplined, responsible, ambitious, professional, manifesting

I resolve/release and/or plan

Tarot, Spell, Oracle, Prayer for First Quarter Phase:

♒ Aquarius 2023

Ephemeris at Midnight UTC

Date	Position
Jan 21 2023	18°Cp10'
Jan 22 2023	03°Aq32'
Jan 23 2023	18°Aq52'
Jan 24 2023	04°Pi00'
Jan 25 2023	18°Pi45'
Jan 26 2023	03°Ar03'
Jan 27 2023	16°Ar50'
Jan 28 2023	00°Ta09'
Jan 29 2023	13°Ta02'
Jan 30 2023	25°Ta35'
Jan 31 2023	07°Ge51'
Feb 1 2023	19°Ge56'
Feb 2 2023	01°Cn53'
Feb 3 2023	13°Cn46'
Feb 4 2023	25°Cn38'
Feb 5 2023	07°Le31'
Feb 6 2023	19°Le25'
Feb 7 2023	01°Vi22'
Feb 8 2023	13°Vi24'
Feb 9 2023	25°Vi32'
Feb 10 2023	07°Li47'
Feb 11 2023	20°Li13'
Feb 12 2023	02°Sc53'
Feb 13 2023	15°Sc50'
Feb 14 2023	29°Sc08'
Feb 15 2023	12°Sg51'
Feb 16 2023	27°Sg00'
Feb 17 2023	11°Cp34'
Feb 18 2023	26°Cp29'
Feb 19 2023	11°Aq39'

1st House: my body, my identity, myself, my appearance, my projected image, my soul-purpose, initial approach to life, my interests, my sense of me
2nd House: my talents, my resources, my physical possessions, my money, my personal self-esteem, my sensuous enjoyment, my self-worth
3rd House: my adaptability, my communications, my siblings, my neighborhood, short journey, my active search for knowledge, learning, curiosity, thinking
4th House: my home, family, heritage, my privacy, my emotional life, feelings, eating habits, receptivity, my protective urges, vulnerability
5th House: my creative abilities, my self-expression pregnancy, children, pleasures, will power, romance, merry making, vacation, affection, confidence
6th House: my work conditions & habits, pets, my health, service offered, productivity, training, work skills, hygiene, clothing, nutrition & diet
7th House: agreements, contracts, partnerships, spouse, relationships, consultants, open enemies, receiving love, self-projection, social skills
8th House: loyalty, partner's money & resources, taxes, inheritance, psychic & occult, transformation, shared values, sexual energy, investigations
9th House: wisdom, justice, law, exploration, faith, religious & spiritual, higher education, foreign travel, legal action, experimentation, truth seeking
10th House: accomplishments, authority, recognition, success, reputation, professional affairs, maturity, proficiency, honor, self-fulfillment, public image/life
11th House: groups & clubs, trends, friends, political awareness, emotional detachment, progressive thought, innovative technology & inventions, astrology
12th House: concern for others, self-sacrifice, psychological health, escapism, drug use, pre-natal imprinting, secret keeping, surrender, spirituality

New

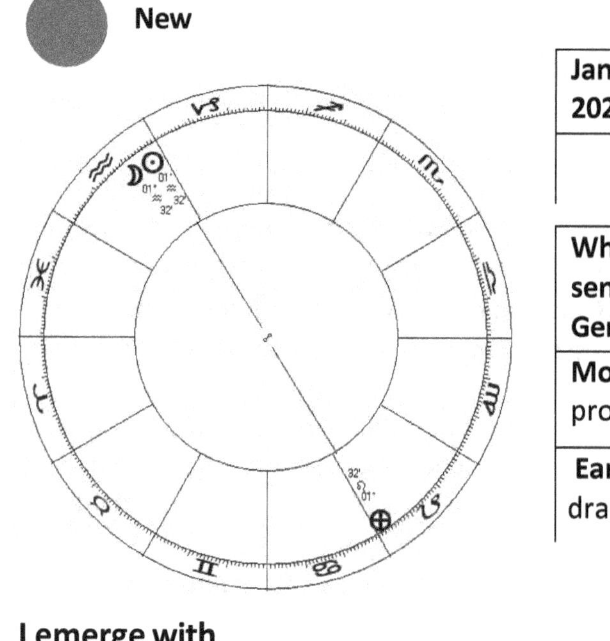

Jan 21 2023	8:53p	Moon 01°♒32'	Earth 01°♌32'	Sun 01°♒32'

What intuitive sense is emerging within me? Where do I sense my emotions in my body? Germination/Seedling/Germination
Moon & Sun in ♒ AQUARIUS: humanitarian, innovative, progressive, eccentric, detached, friendly, generous
Earth in ♌ LEO: self-confident, generous, playful, dramatic, courageous, caring, brave, self-centered

I emerge with

Tarot, Spell, Oracle, Prayer for Crescent Phase:

Crescent Moon

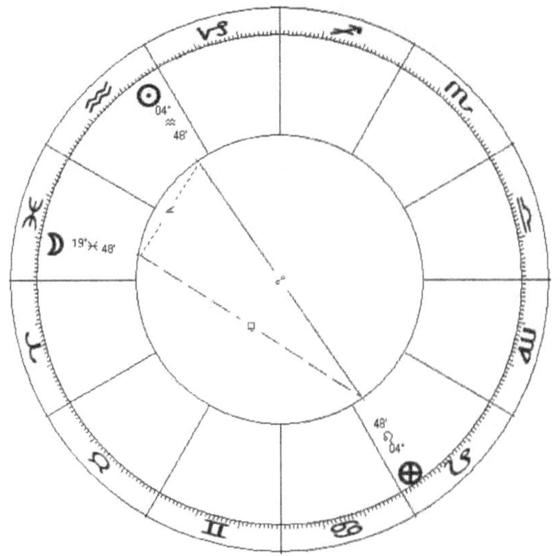

Jan 25 2023	1:42a	Moon 19°♓48'	Earth 04°♌48'	Sun 04°♒48'

What is my challenge? What is my promise? Is my ego an asset or liability? Sprout
Moon in ♓ PISCES: spiritual, subtle, empathic, psychic, vulnerable, intuitive, self- sacrificing, artistic
Earth in ♌ LEO: self-confident, generous, playful, dramatic, courageous, caring, brave, self-centered
Sun in ♒ AQUARIUS: humanitarian, innovative, progressive, eccentric, detached, friendly, generous

I challenge myself to

Tarot, Spell, Oracle, Prayer for Crescent Phase:

First Quarter

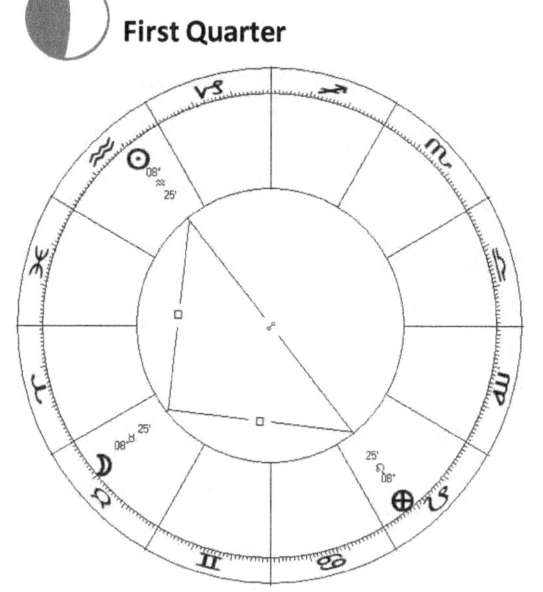

Jan 28 2023	3:18p	Moon 08° ♉ 25'	Earth 08° ♌ 25'	Sun 08° ♒ 25'

What steps will I take toward accomplishing my goals? How do I move forward? Root/Stem/Leaf - photosynthesis
Moon in ♉ TAURUS: sensual, dependable, resourceful, deliberate, practical, comfortable, stubborn
Earth in ♌ LEO: self-confident, generous, playful, dramatic, courageous, caring, brave, self-centered
Sun in ♒ AQUARIUS: humanitarian, innovative, progressive, eccentric, detached, friendly, generous

I take action on

Tarot, Spell, Oracle, Prayer for First Quarter Phase:

Gibbous

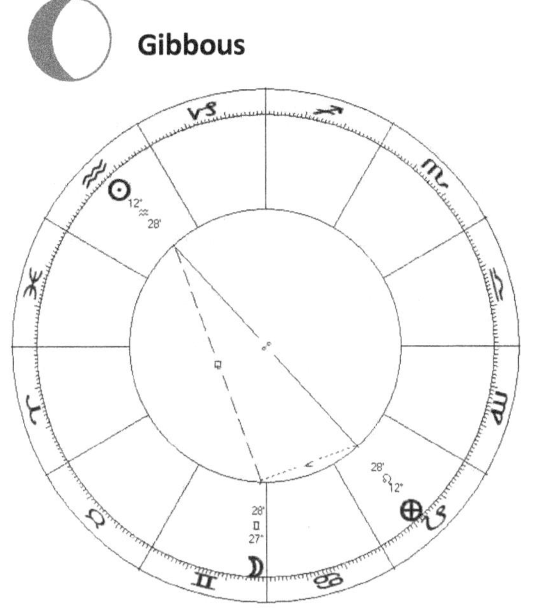

Feb 1 2023	3:07p	Moon 27° ♊ 28'	Earth 12° ♌ 28'	Sun 12° ♒ 28'

How do I stay on track? What do I need to stay organized? What do I need to compromise? Buds appear and develop in size.
Moon in ♊ GEMINI: Clever, versatile, curious, articulate, adaptable, lighthearted, quick-witted, cheerful, talkative
Earth in ♌ LEO: self-confident, generous, playful, dramatic, courageous, caring, brave, self-centered
Sun in ♒ AQUARIUS: humanitarian, innovative, progressive, eccentric, detached, friendly, generous

I develop structure with

Tarot, Spell, Oracle, Prayer for Gibbous Phase:

Full

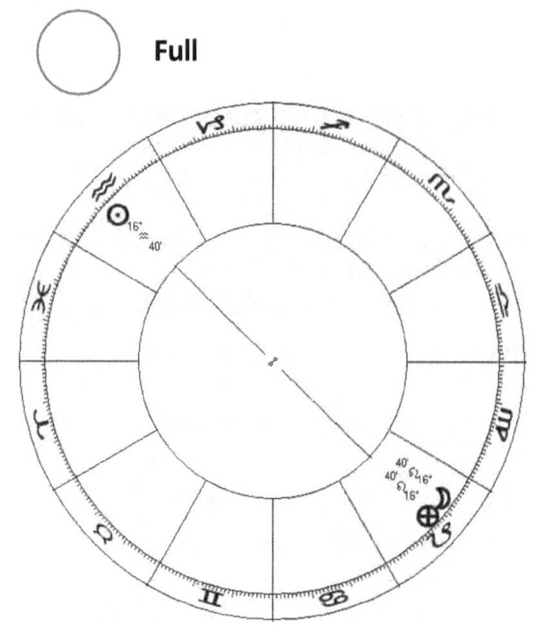

Feb 5 2023	6:28p	Moon 16°♌40'	Earth 16°♎ 40'	Sun 16°♒40'

How do function in my world with my process? What does it look like in my day-to-day world? Flower/Fruit
Moon & Earth in ♌ LEO: self-confident, generous, playful, dramatic, courageous, caring, brave, self-centered
Sun in ♒ AQUARIUS: humanitarian, innovative, progressive, eccentric, detached, friendly, generous

I communicate my commitment to

Tarot, Spell, Oracle, Prayer for Full Moon Phase:

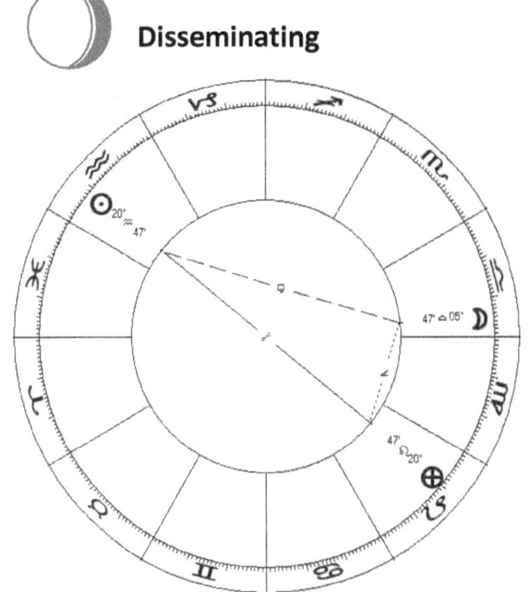

Disseminating

Feb 9 2023	8:07p	Moon 05°♎48'	Earth 20°♌47'	Sun 20°♒47'

How can I share my experiences? How can I help others with my learning and experience? First harvest.
Moon in ♎ LIBRA: cooperative, fair, considerate, artistic, diplomatic, tactful, impartial, refined
Earth in ♌ LEO: self-confident, generous, playful, dramatic, courageous, caring, brave, self-centered
Sun in ♒ AQUARIUS: humanitarian, innovative, progressive, eccentric, detached, friendly, generous

I share

Tarot, Spell, Oracle, Prayer for Disseminating Phase:

Last Quarter

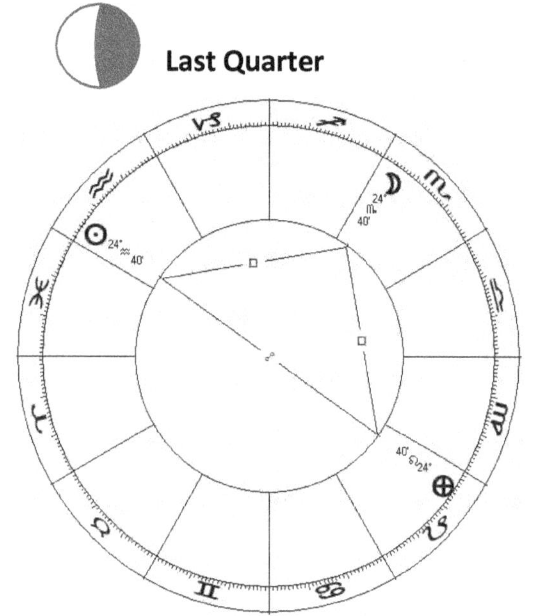

Feb 13 2023	4:00p	Moon 24°♏40'	Earth 24°♌40'	Sun 24°♒40'

How do I change- let go of the patterns that do not serve me and/or my community? Decay/Last Harvest & composting.
Moon in ♏ SCORPIO: transformative, sexual, secretive, musical, trust-worthy, loyal, supportive, jealous
Earth in ♌ LEO: self-confident, generous, playful, dramatic, courageous, caring, brave, self-centered
Sun in ♒ AQUARIUS: humanitarian, innovative, progressive, eccentric, detached, friendly, generous

I change perspective on

Tarot, Spell, Oracle, Prayer for Last Quarter Phase:

Balsamic

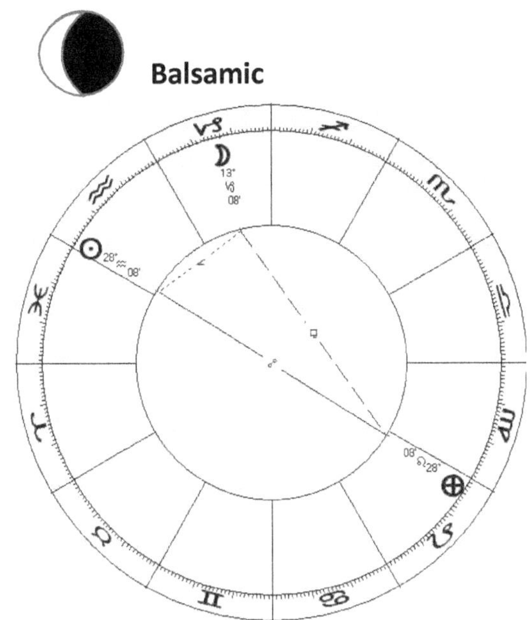

Feb 17 2023	2:33a	Moon 13°♑08'	Earth 28°♌08'	Sun 28°♒08'

How do I resolve this cycle & visualize, plan? Seed is planted, released to create next cycle/ germination begins.
Moon in ♑ CAPRICORN: disciplined, responsible, ambitious, professional**,** manifesting
Earth in ♌ LEO: self-confident, generous, playful, dramatic, courageous, caring, brave, self-centered
Sun in ♒ AQUARIUS: humanitarian, innovative, progressive, eccentric, detached, friendly, generous

I resolve/release and/or plan

Tarot, Spell, Oracle, Prayer for Balsamic Phase:

♓ Pisces 2023

Ephemeris at Midnight UTC

Date	Position
Feb 20 2023	**26°Aq52'**
Feb 21 2023	**11°Pi59'**
Feb 22 2023	**26°Pi49'**
Feb 23 2023	**11°Ar14'**
Feb 24 2023	**25°Ar11'**
Feb 25 2023	**08°Ta38'**
Feb 26 2023	**21°Ta39'**
Feb 27 2023	**04°Ge16'**
Feb 28 2023	**16°Ge35'**
Mar 1 2023	**28°Ge40'**
Mar 2 2023	**10°Cn36'**
Mar 3 2023	**22°Cn27'**
Mar 4 2023	**04°Le19'**
Mar 5 2023	**16°Le12'**
Mar 6 2023	**28°Le10'**
Mar 7 2023	**10°Vi14'**
Mar 8 2023	**22°Vi26'**
Mar 9 2023	**04°Li46'**
Mar 10 2023	**17°Li16'**
Mar 11 2023	**29°Li56'**
Mar 12 2023	**12°Sc49'**
Mar 13 2023	**25°Sc56'**
Mar 14 2023	**09°Sg18'**
Mar 15 2023	**22°Sg59'**
Mar 16 2023	**06°Cp58'**
Mar 17 2023	**21°Cp16'**
Mar 18 2023	**05°Aq50'**
Mar 19 2023	**20°Aq36'**
Mar 20 2023	**05°Pi26'**

1st House: my body, my identity, myself, my appearance, my projected image, my soul-purpose, initial approach to life, my interests, my sense of me

2nd House: my talents, my resources, my physical possessions, my money, my personal self-esteem, my sensuous enjoyment, my self-worth

3rd House: my adaptability, my communications, my siblings, my neighborhood, short journey, my active search for knowledge, learning, curiosity, thinking

4th House: my home, family, heritage, my privacy, my emotional life, feelings, eating habits, receptivity, my protective urges, vulnerability

5th House: my creative abilities, my self-expression pregnancy, children, pleasures, will power, romance, merry making, vacation, affection, confidence

6th House: my work conditions & habits, pets, my health, service offered, productivity, training, work skills, hygiene, clothing, nutrition & diet

7th House: agreements, contracts, partnerships, spouse, relationships, consultants, open enemies, receiving love, self-projection, social skills

8th House: loyalty, partner's money & resources, taxes, inheritance, psychic & occult, transformation, shared values, sexual energy, investigations

9th House: wisdom, justice, law, exploration, faith, religious & spiritual, higher education, foreign travel, legal action, experimentation, truth seeking

10th House: accomplishments, authority, recognition, success, reputation, professional affairs, maturity, proficiency, honor, self-fulfillment, public image/life

11th House: groups & clubs, trends, friends, political awareness, emotional detachment, progressive thought, innovative technology & inventions, astrology

12th House: concern for others, self-sacrifice, psychological health, escapism, drug use, pre-natal imprinting, secret keeping, surrender, spirituality

New

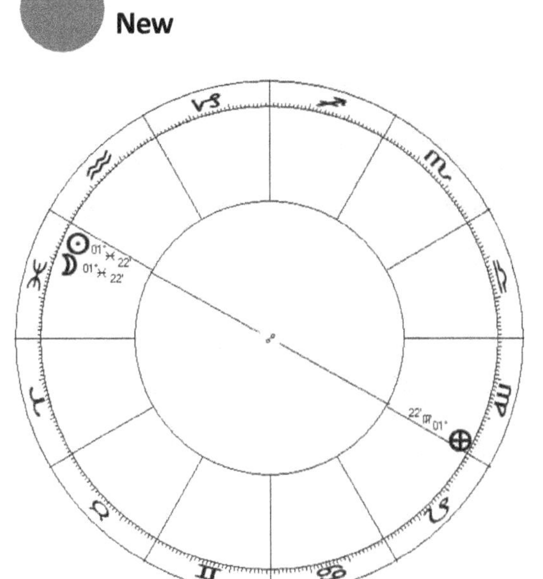

Feb 20 2023	7:05a	Moon 01°♓22'	Earth 01°♍22'	Sun 01°♓22'

What intuitive sense is emerging within me? Where do I sense my emotions in my body? Germination/Seedling/Germination
Moon & Sun ♓ PISCES: spiritual, subtle, empathic, psychic, vulnerable, intuitive, self- sacrificing, artistic
Earth in ♍ VIRGO: analytical, efficient, healing health-conscious, exacting, technical

I emerge with

Tarot, Spell, Oracle, Prayer for New Moon Phase:

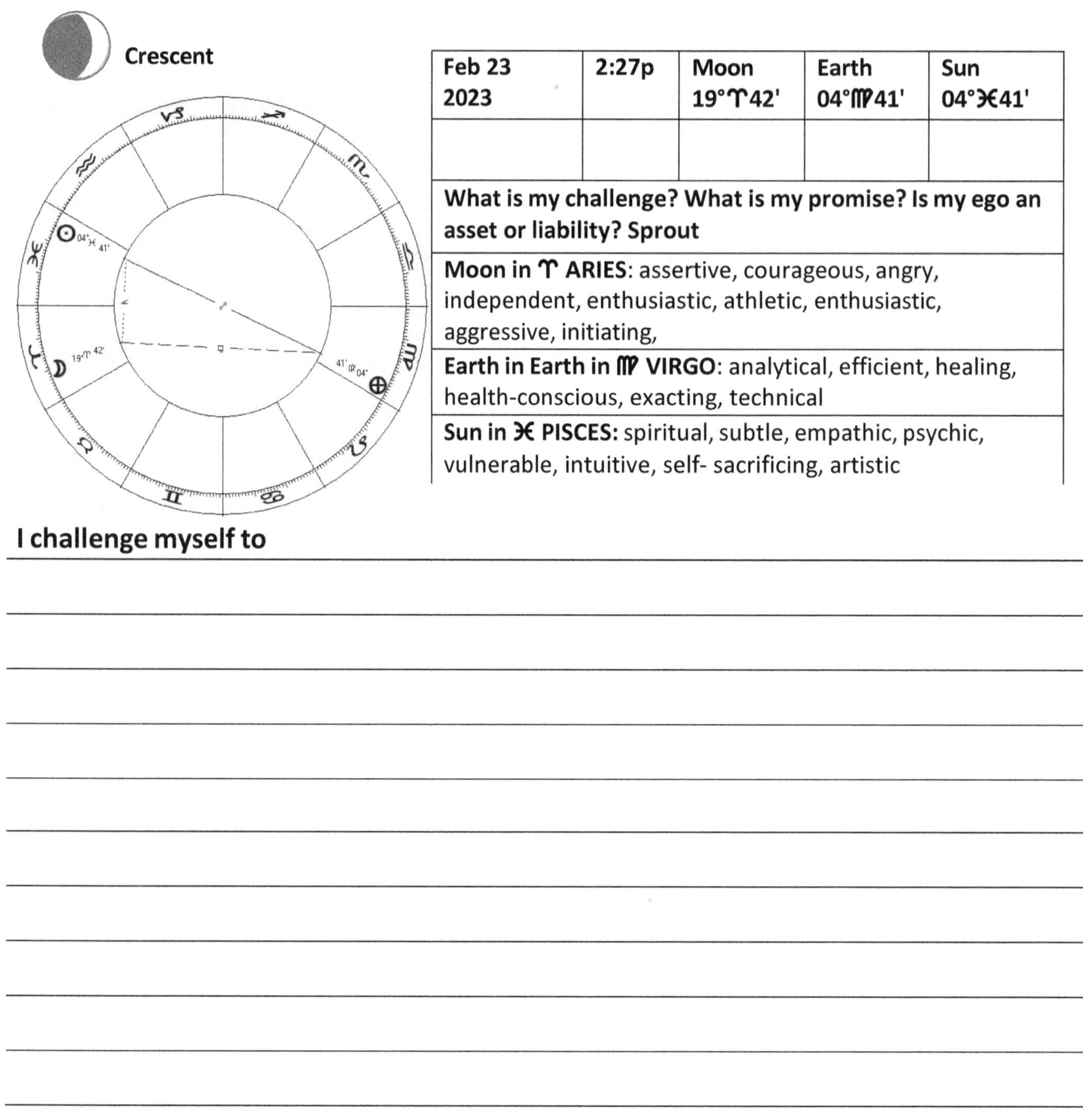

Crescent

Feb 23 2023	2:27p	Moon 19°♈42'	Earth 04°♍41'	Sun 04°♓41'
What is my challenge? What is my promise? Is my ego an asset or liability? Sprout				
Moon in ♈ ARIES: assertive, courageous, angry, independent, enthusiastic, athletic, enthusiastic, aggressive, initiating,				
Earth in Earth in ♍ VIRGO: analytical, efficient, healing, health-conscious, exacting, technical				
Sun in ♓ PISCES: spiritual, subtle, empathic, psychic, vulnerable, intuitive, self- sacrificing, artistic				

I challenge myself to

Tarot, Spell, Oracle, Prayer for Crescent Phase

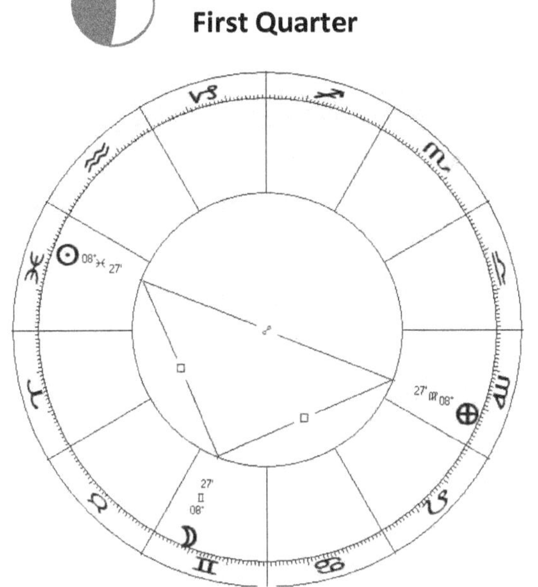

First Quarter

Feb 27 023	8:05a	Moon 08°♊27'	Earth 08°♍27'	Sun 08°♓27'

What steps will I take toward accomplishing my goals? How do I move forward? Root/Stem/Leaf - photosynthesis
Moon in ♊ GEMINI: Clever, versatile, curious, articulate, adaptable, lighthearted, quick-witted, cheerful, talkative
Earth in ♍ VIRGO: analytical, efficient, healing health-conscious, exacting, technical
Sun in ♓ PISCES: spiritual, subtle, empathic, psychic, vulnerable, intuitive, self- sacrificing, artistic

I take action on

Tarot, Spell, Oracle, Prayer for First Quarter Phase:

Gibbous

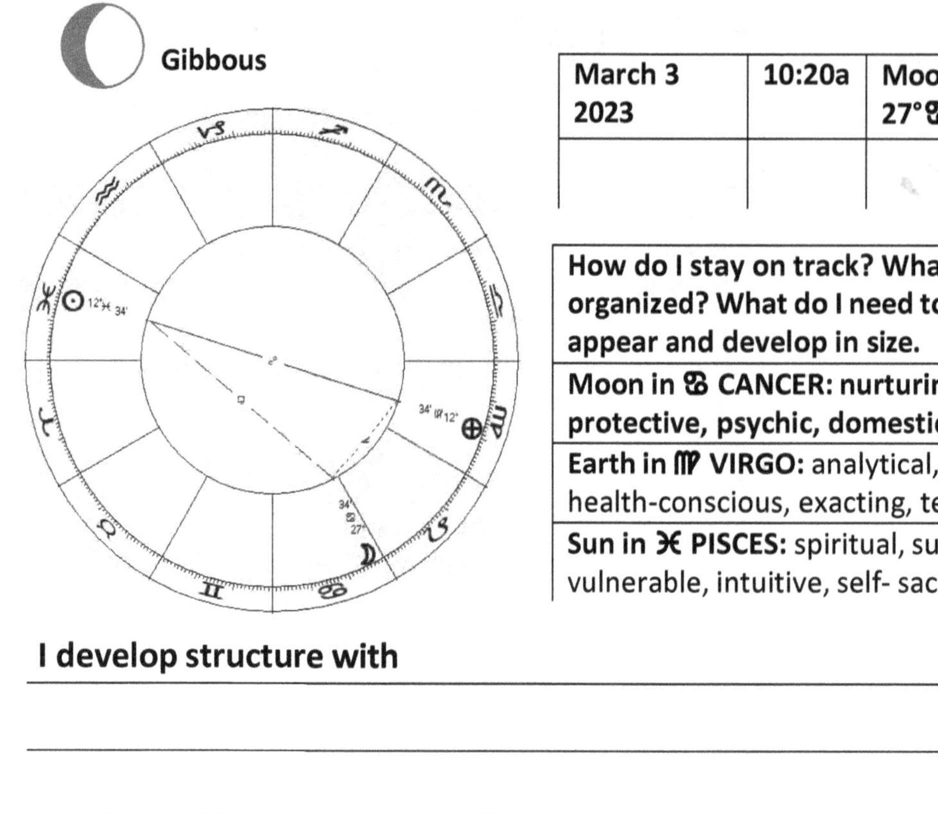

March 3 2023	10:20a	Moon 27°♋34'	Earth 12°♍34'	Sun 12°♓34'

How do I stay on track? What do I need to stay organized? What do I need to compromise? Buds appear and develop in size.
Moon in ♋ CANCER: nurturing, attached, emotional, protective, psychic, domestic, intuitive
Earth in ♍ VIRGO: analytical, efficient, healing health-conscious, exacting, technical
Sun in ♓ PISCES: spiritual, subtle, empathic, psychic, vulnerable, intuitive, self- sacrificing, artistic

I develop structure with

Tarot, Spell, Oracle, Prayer for Gibbous Phase

Full

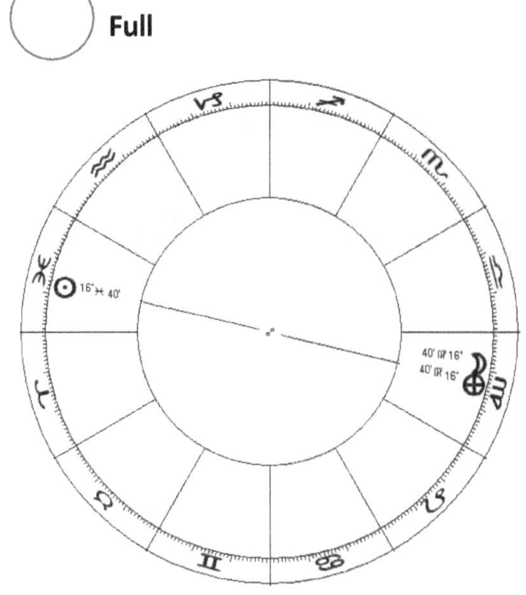

March 7 2023	12:40p	Moon 16°♍40'	Earth 16°♍40'	Sun 16°♓40'

How do function in my world with my process? What does it look like in my day-to-day world? Flower/Fruit
Moon & Earth in ♍ VIRGO: analytical, efficient, healing health-conscious, exacting, technical
Sun in ♓ PISCES: spiritual, subtle, empathic, psychic, vulnerable, intuitive, self- sacrificing, artistic

I communicate my commitment to

Tarot, Spell, Oracle, Prayer for Full Moon Phase:

Disseminating

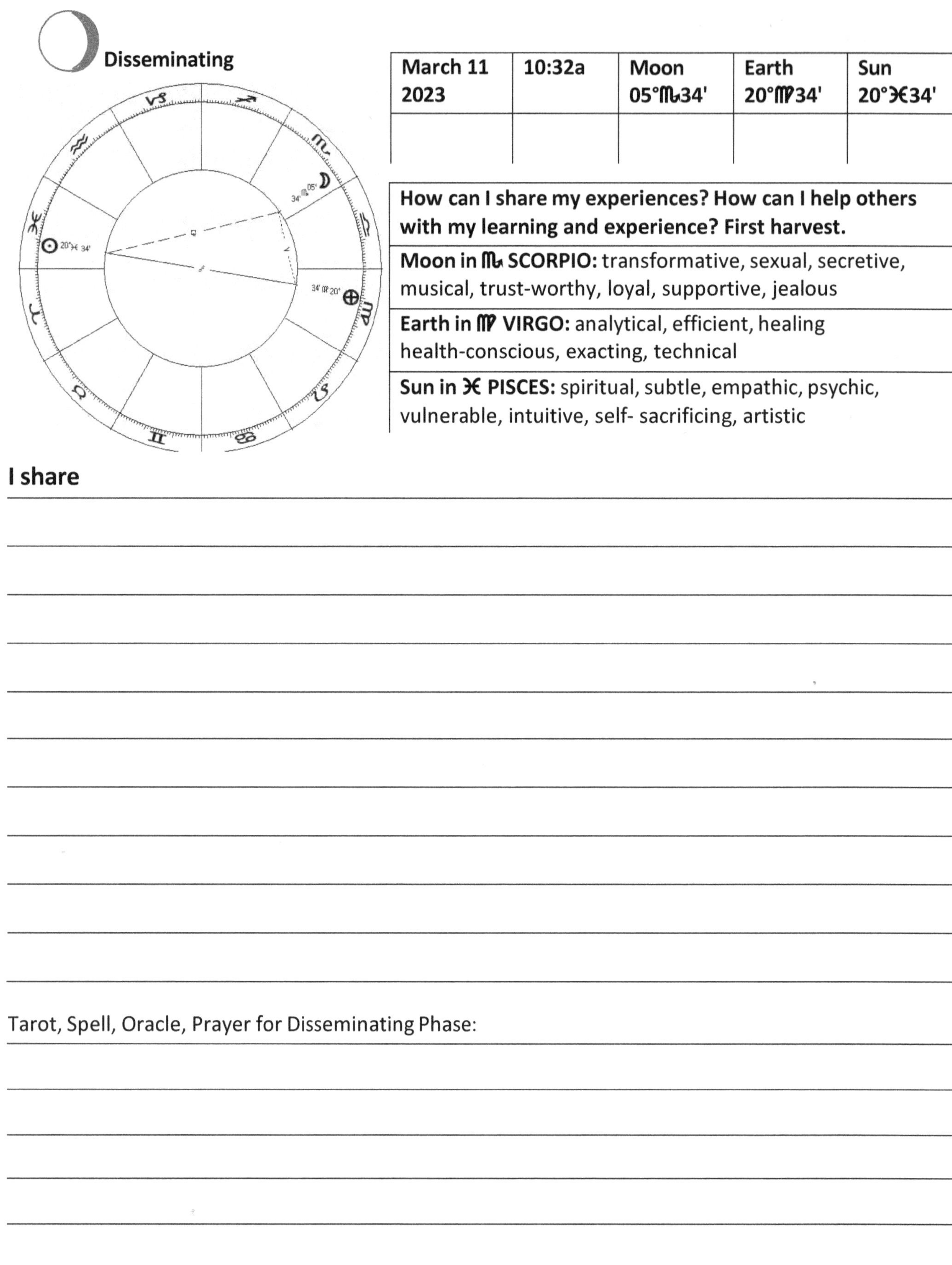

March 11 2023	10:32a	Moon 05°♏34'	Earth 20°♍34'	Sun 20°♓34'

How can I share my experiences? How can I help others with my learning and experience? First harvest.
Moon in ♏ SCORPIO: transformative, sexual, secretive, musical, trust-worthy, loyal, supportive, jealous
Earth in ♍ VIRGO: analytical, efficient, healing health-conscious, exacting, technical
Sun in ♓ PISCES: spiritual, subtle, empathic, psychic, vulnerable, intuitive, self- sacrificing, artistic

I share

Tarot, Spell, Oracle, Prayer for Disseminating Phase:

Last Quarter

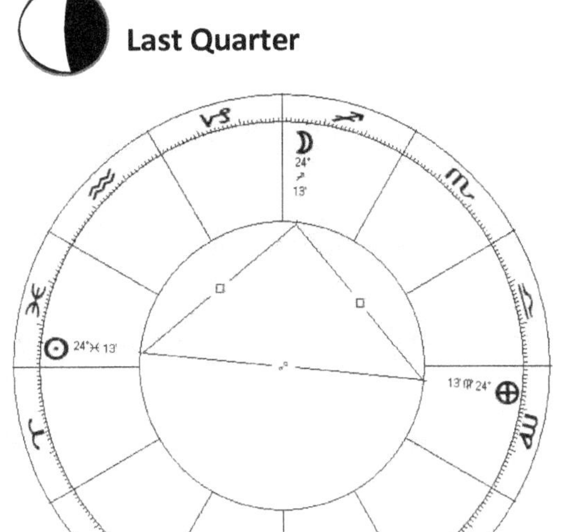

March 15 2023	2:08a	Moon 24°♐13'	Earth 24 °♍13'	Sun 24°♓13'

How do I change- let go of the patterns that do not serve me and/or my community? Decay/Last Harvest & composting.
Moon in ♐SAGITTARIUS: philosophical, truth seeking, ethical, idealistic, optimistic, inspiring, wise, motivational, honest
Earth in ♍ VIRGO: analytical, efficient, healing health-conscious, exacting, technical
Sun in ♓ PISCES: spiritual, subtle, empathic, psychic, vulnerable, intuitive, self- sacrificing, artistic

I change perspective on

Tarot, Spell, Oracle, Prayer for Last Quarter Phase:

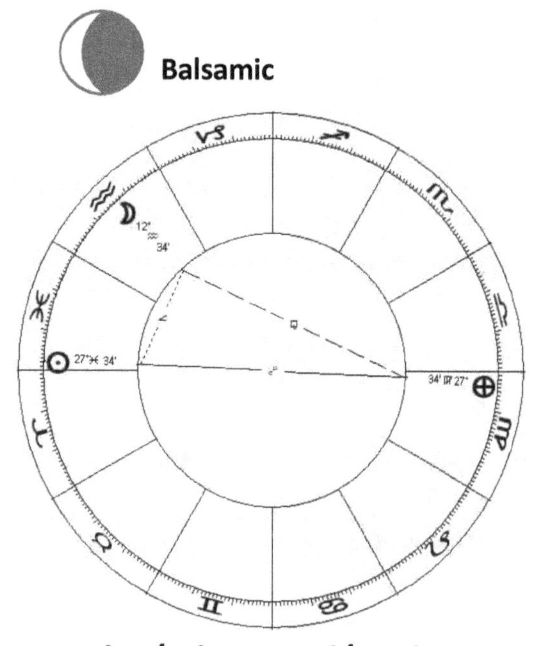

Balsamic

March 18 2023	10:58a	Moon 12°♒34'	Earth 27°♍34'	Sun 27°♓34'

How do I resolve this cycle & visualize, plan? Seed is planted, released to create next cycle/ germination begins.
Moon in ♒ AQUARIUS: humanitarian, innovative, progressive, eccentric, detached, friendly, generous
Earth in ♍ VIRGO: analytical, efficient, healing health-conscious, exacting, technical
Sun in ♓PISCES: spiritual, subtle, empathic, psychic, vulnerable, intuitive, self- sacrificing, artistic

I resolve/release and/or plan

Tarot, Spell, Oracle, Prayer for Balsamic Phase:

♈ Aries 2023 #1

Ephemeris at Midnight UTC

Date	Position
Mar 21 2023	20°Pi13'
Mar 22 2023	04°Ar49'
Mar 23 2023	19°Ar07'
Mar 24 2023	03°Ta02'
Mar 25 2023	16°Ta32'
Mar 26 2023	29°Ta37'
Mar 27 2023	12°Ge20'
Mar 28 2023	24°Ge43'
Mar 29 2023	06°Cn52'
Mar 30 2023	18°Cn50'
Mar 31 2023	00°Le43'
Apr 1 2023	12°Le36'
Apr 2 2023	24°Le31'
Apr 3 2023	06°Vi33'
Apr 4 2023	18°Vi44'
Apr 5 2023	01°Li06'
Apr 6 2023	13°Li41'
Apr 7 2023	26°Li30'
Apr 8 2023	09°Sc31'
Apr 9 2023	22°Sc46'
Apr 10 2023	06°Sg13'
Apr 11 2023	19°Sg53'
Apr 12 2023	03°Cp44'
Apr 13 2023	17°Cp46'
Apr 14 2023	01°Aq57'
Apr 15 2023	16°Aq15'
Apr 16 2023	00°Pi37'
Apr 17 2023	15°Pi00'
Apr 18 2023	29°Pi18'
Apr 19 2023	13°Ar28'

1st House: my body, my identity, myself, my appearance, my projected image, my soul-purpose, initial approach to life, my interests, my sense of me
2nd House: my talents, my resources, my physical possessions, my money, my personal self-esteem, my sensuous enjoyment, my self-worth
3rd House: my adaptability, my communications, my siblings, my neighborhood, short journey, my active search for knowledge, learning, curiosity, thinking
4th House: my home, family, heritage, my privacy, my emotional life, feelings, eating habits, receptivity, my protective urges, vulnerability
5th House: my creative abilities, my self-expression pregnancy, children, pleasures, will power, romance, merry making, vacation, affection, confidence
6th House: my work conditions & habits, pets, my health, service offered, productivity, training, work skills, hygiene, clothing, nutrition & diet
7th House: agreements, contracts, partnerships, spouse, relationships, consultants, open enemies, receiving love, self-projection, social skills
8th House: loyalty, partner's money & resources, taxes, inheritance, psychic & occult, transformation, shared values, sexual energy, investigations
9th House: wisdom, justice, law, exploration, faith, religious & spiritual, higher education, foreign travel, legal action, experimentation, truth seeking
10th House: accomplishments, authority, recognition, success, reputation, professional affairs, maturity, proficiency, honor, self-fulfillment, public image/life
11th House: groups & clubs, trends, friends, political awareness, emotional detachment, progressive thought, innovative technology & inventions, astrology
12th House: concern for others, self-sacrifice, psychological health, escapism, drug use, pre-natal imprinting, secret keeping, surrender, spirituality

New Moon

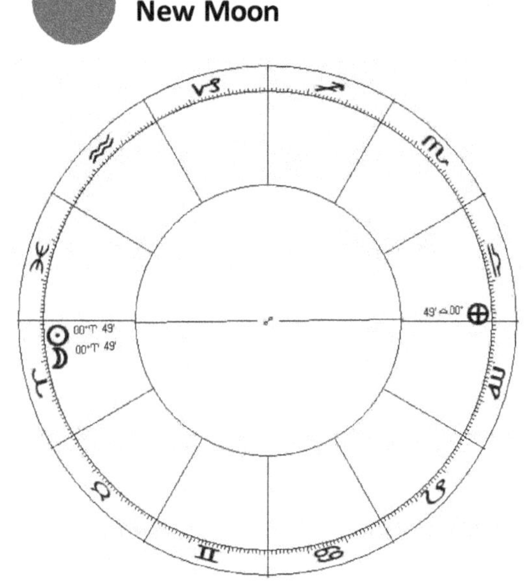

March 21 2023	5:23p	Moon 00°♈49'	Earth 00°♎49'	Sun 00°♈49'

What intuitive sense is emerging within me? Where do I sense my emotions in my body? Germination/Seedling/Germination
Moon & Sun in ♈ ARIES: assertive, courageous, independent, enthusiastic, athletic, enthusiastic, aggressive, initiating, angry
Earth in ♎ LIBRA: cooperative, fair, considerate, artistic, diplomatic, tactful, impartial, refined

I emerge with

Tarot, Spell, Oracle, Prayer for New Moon Phase:

Crescent

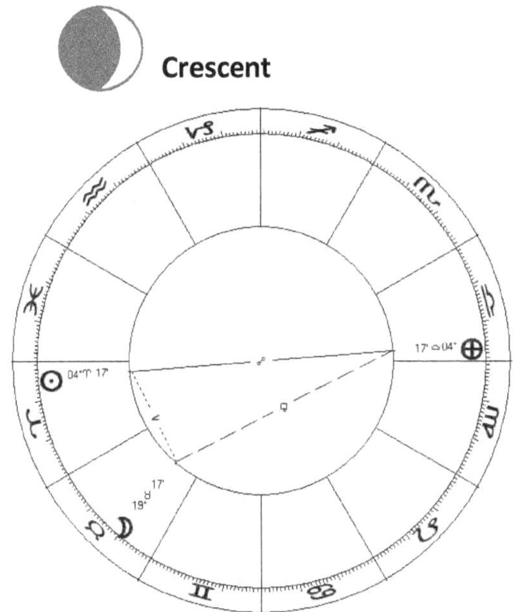

March 25 2023	4:58a	Moon 19° ♉ 17'	Earth 04° ♎ 17'	Sun 04° ♈ 17'

What is my challenge? What is my promise? Is my ego an asset or liability? Sprout
Moon in ♉ TAURUS: sensual, dependable, resourceful, deliberate, practical, comfortable, stubborn
Earth in ♎ LIBRA: cooperative, fair, considerate, artistic, diplomatic, tactful, impartial, refined
Sun in ♈ ARIES: assertive, courageous, independent, enthusiastic, athletic, enthusiastic, aggressive, initiating, angry

I challenge myself to

Tarot, Spell, Oracle, Prayer for Crescent Phase:

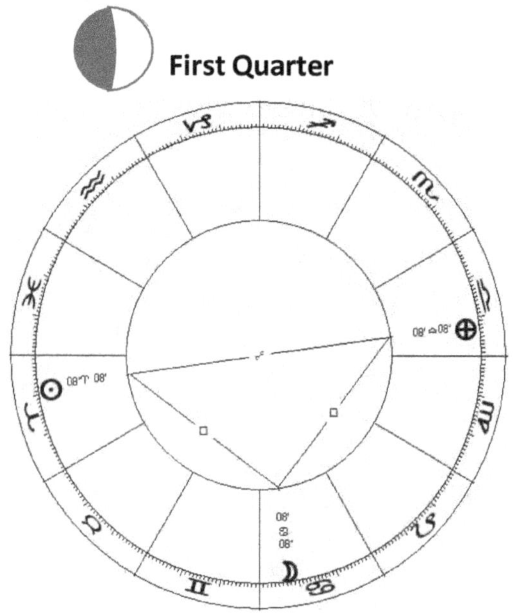

First Quarter

March 29 2023	2:32a	Moon 08°♋08'	Earth 08°♎08'	Sun 08°♈08'
What steps will I take toward accomplishing my goals? How do I move forward? Root/Stem/Leaf - photosynthesis				
Moon in ♋ CANCER: nurturing, attached, emotional, protective, psychic, domestic, intuitive				
Earth in ♎ LIBRA: cooperative, fair, considerate, artistic, diplomatic, tactful, impartial, refined				
Sun in ♈ ARIES: assertive, courageous, independent, enthusiastic, athletic, enthusiastic, aggressive, initiating, angry				

I take action on

Tarot, Spell, Oracle, Prayer for First Quarter Phase:

Gibbous

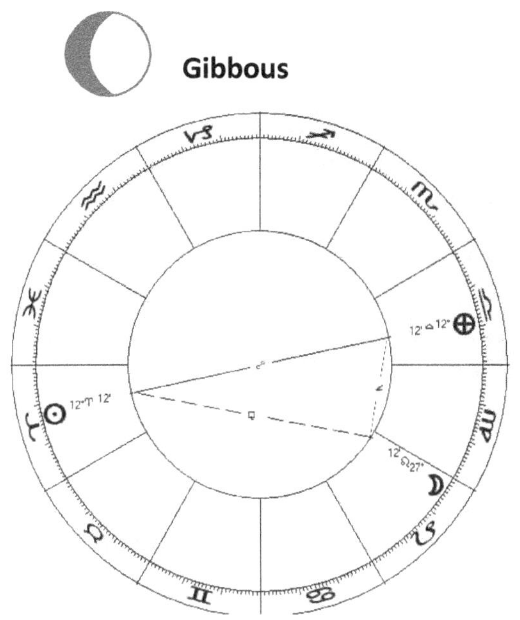

Apr 2 2023	5:23a	Moon 27°♌12'	Earth 12°♎12'	Sun 12°♈12'
How do I stay on track? What do I need to stay organized? What do I need to compromise? Buds appear and develop in size.				
Moon in ♌ LEO: self-confident, generous, playful, dramatic, courageous, caring, brave, self-centered				
Earth in ♎ LIBRA: cooperative, fair, considerate, artistic, diplomatic, tactful, impartial, refined				
Sun in ♈ ARIES: assertive, courageous, independent, enthusiastic, athletic, enthusiastic, aggressive, initiating, angry				

I develop structure with

Tarot, Spell, Oracle, Prayer for Gibbous Phase:

Full

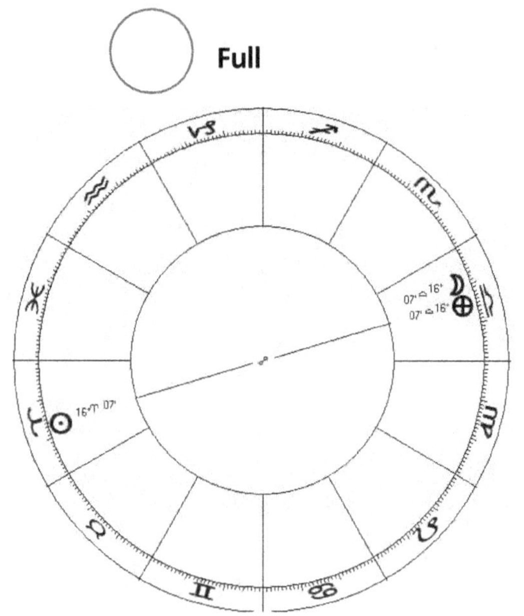

April 6 2023	4:34a	Moon 16°♎07'	Earth 16°♎07'	Sun 16°♈07'

How do function in my world with my process? What does it look like in my day-to-day world? Flower/Fruit
Moon in ♎ LIBRA: cooperative, fair, considerate, artistic, diplomatic, tactful, impartial, refined
Earth in ♎ LIBRA: cooperative, fair, considerate, artistic, diplomatic, tactful, impartial, refined
Sun in ♈ ARIES: assertive, courageous, independent, enthusiastic, athletic, enthusiastic, aggressive, initiating, angry

I communicate my commitment to

Tarot, Spell, Oracle, Prayer for Full Moon Phase:

Disseminating

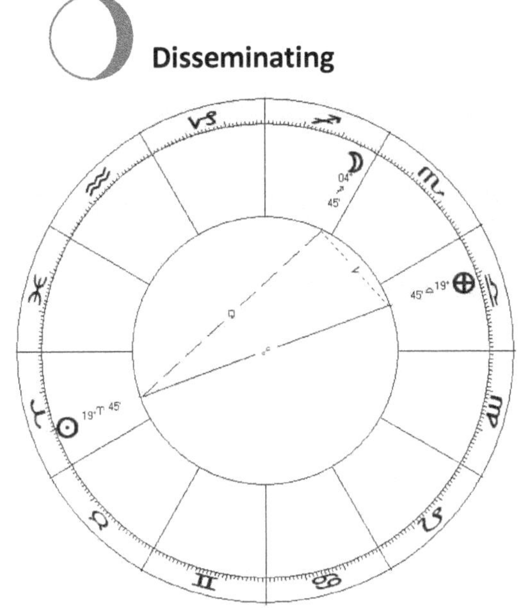

April 9 2023	9:24p	Moon 04°♐45'	Earth 19°♎45'	Sun 19°♈45'

How can I share my experiences? How can I help others with my learning and experience? First harvest.
Moon in ♐ SAGITTARIUS: philosophical, truth-seeking, ethical, idealistic, optimistic, inspiring, wise, honest
Earth in ♎ LIBRA: cooperative, fair, considerate, artistic, diplomatic, tactful, impartial, refined
Sun in ♈ ARIES: assertive, courageous, independent, enthusiastic, athletic, enthusiastic, aggressive, initiating, angry

I share

Tarot, Spell, Oracle, Prayer for Disseminating Phase:

Last Quarter

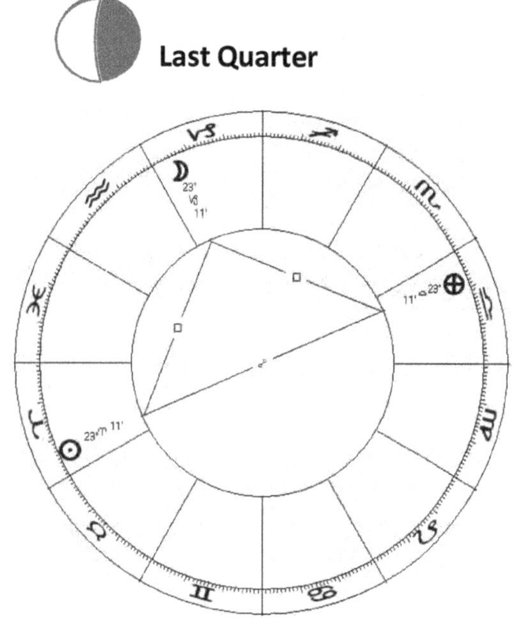

April 13 2023	9:11a	Moon 23°♑11'	Earth 23°♎11'	Sun 23°♈11

How do I change- let go of the patterns that do not serve me and/or my community? Decay/Last Harvest & composting.
Moon in ♑CAPRICORN: disciplined, responsible, ambitious, professional, manifesting
Earth in ♎ LIBRA: cooperative, fair, considerate, artistic, diplomatic, tactful, impartial, refined
Sun in ♈ ARIES: assertive, courageous, independent, enthusiastic, athletic, enthusiastic, aggressive, initiating, angry

I change perspective on

Tarot, Spell, Oracle, Prayer for Last Quarter Phase:

Balsamic

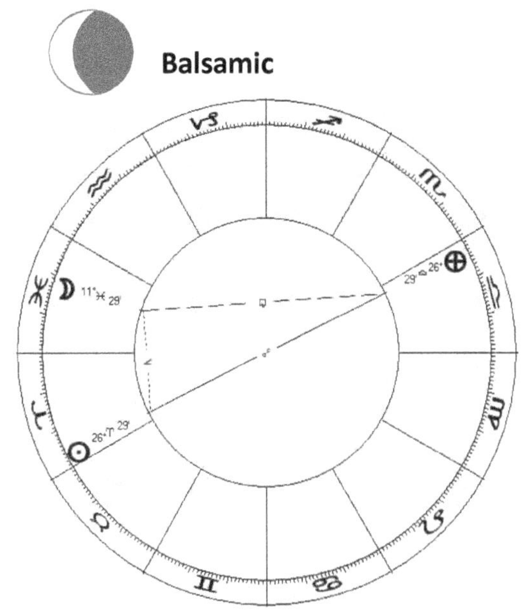

April 16 2023	6:07p	Moon 11 °♓29'	Earth 26°♎29'	Sun 26°♈29'

How do I resolve this cycle & visualize, plan? Seed is planted, released to create next cycle/ germination begins.
Moon in ♓ PISCES: spiritual, subtle, empathic, psychic, vulnerable, intuitive, self- sacrificing, artistic
Earth in ♎ LIBRA: cooperative, fair, considerate, artistic, diplomatic, tactful, impartial, refined
Sun in ♈ ARIES: assertive, courageous, independent, enthusiastic, athletic, enthusiastic, aggressive, initiating, angry

I resolve/release and/or plan

Tarot, Spell, Oracle, Prayer for Balsamic Phase:

♈ Aries 2023 #2

Ephemeris at Midnight UTC

Date	Position
Apr 20 2023	**27°Ar25'**
Apr 21 2023	**11°Ta05'**
Apr 22 2023	**24°Ta26'**
Apr 23 2023	**07°Ge27'**
Apr 24 2023	**20°Ge09'**
Apr 25 2023	**02°Cn34'**
Apr 26 2023	**14°Cn45'**
Apr 27 2023	**26°Cn46'**
Apr 28 2023	**08°Le40'**
Apr 29 2023	**20°Le33'**
Apr 30 2023	**02°Vi30'**
May 1 2023	**14°Vi33'**
May 2 2023	**26°Vi49'**
May 3 2023	**09°Li19'**
May 4 2023	**22°Li06'**
May 5 2023	**05°Sc11'**
May 6 2023	**18°Sc35'**
May 7 2023	**02°Sg15'**
May 8 2023	**16°Sg10'**
May 9 2023	**00°Cp16'**
May 10 2023	**14°Cp28'**
May 11 2023	**28°Cp45'**
May 12 2023	**13°Aq01'**
May 13 2023	**27°Aq15'**
May 14 2023	**11°Pi23'**
May 15 2023	**25°Pi24'**
May 16 2023	**09°Ar16'**
May 17 2023	**22°Ar57'**
May 18 2023	**06°Ta28'**

1st House: my body, my identity, myself, my appearance, my projected image, my soul-purpose, initial approach to life, my interests, my sense of me
2nd House: my talents, my resources, my physical possessions, my money, my personal self-esteem, my sensuous enjoyment, my self-worth
3rd House: my adaptability, my communications, my siblings, my neighborhood, short journey, my active search for knowledge, learning, curiosity, thinking
4th House: my home, family, heritage, my privacy, my emotional life, feelings, eating habits, receptivity, my protective urges, vulnerability
5th House: my creative abilities, my self-expression pregnancy, children, pleasures, will power, romance, merry making, vacation, affection, confidence
6th House: my work conditions & habits, pets, my health, service offered, productivity, training, work skills, hygiene, clothing, nutrition & diet
7th House: agreements, contracts, partnerships, spouse, relationships, consultants, open enemies, receiving love, self-projection, social skills
8th House: loyalty, partner's money & resources, taxes, inheritance, psychic & occult, transformation, shared values, sexual energy, investigations
9th House: wisdom, justice, law, exploration, faith, religious & spiritual, higher education, foreign travel, legal action, experimentation, truth seeking
10th House: accomplishments, authority, recognition, success, reputation, professional affairs, maturity, proficiency, honor, self-fulfillment, public image/life
11th House: groups & clubs, trends, friends, political awareness, emotional detachment, progressive thought, innovative technology & inventions, astrology
12th House: concern for others, self-sacrifice, psychological health, escapism, drug use, pre-natal imprinting, secret keeping, surrender, spirituality

New Moon – Solar Hybrid Eclipse

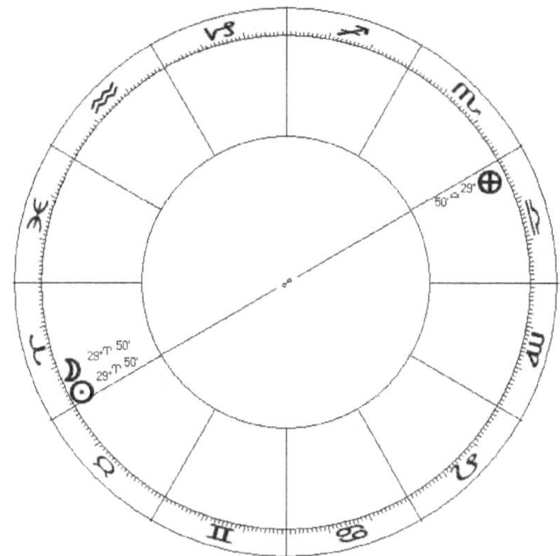

April 20 2023	4:12a	Moon 29°♈50'	Earth 29°♎50'	Sun 29°♈50'

What intuitive sense is emerging within me? Where do I sense my emotions in my body? Germination/Seedling/Germination

Moon & Sun in ♈ ARIES: assertive, courageous, independent, enthusiastic, athletic, enthusiastic, aggressive, initiating, angry

Earth in ♎ LIBRA: cooperative, fair, considerate, artistic, diplomatic, tactful, impartial, refined

I emerge with

Tarot, Spell, Oracle, Prayer for New Moon Phase:

Crescent

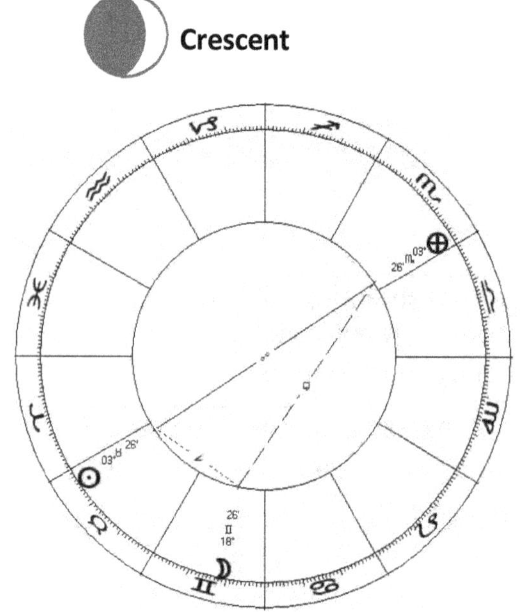

April 23 2023	8:42p	Moon 18° ♊ 26'	Earth 03°♏26'	Sun 03° ♉ 26'

What is my challenge? What is my promise? Is my ego an asset or liability? Sprout
Moon in ♊ GEMINI: Clever, versatile, curious, articulate, adaptable, lighthearted, quick-witted, cheerful
Earth in ♏ SCORPIO: transformative, sexual, secretive, musical, trust-worthy, loyal, supportive, jealous
Sun in ♉ TAURUS: sensual, dependable, resourceful, deliberate, practical, comfortable, stubborn

I challenge myself to

Tarot, Spell, Oracle, Prayer for Crescent Phase:

First Quarter

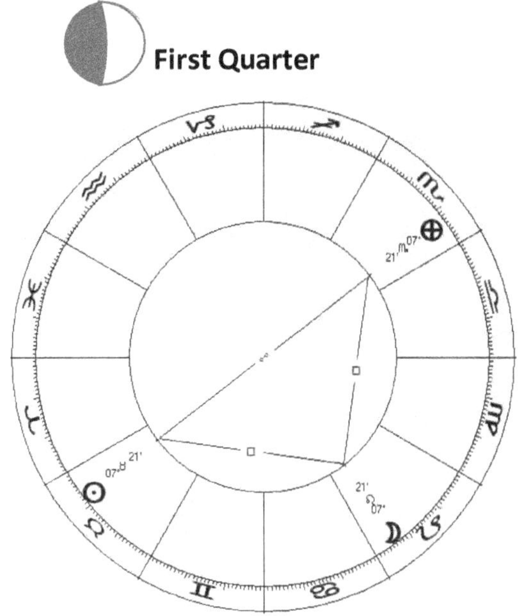

April 27 2023	9:19p	Moon 07°♌21'	Earth 07°♏21'	Sun 07°♉21'

What steps will I take toward accomplishing my goals? How do I move forward? Root/Stem/Leaf - photosynthesis
Moon in ♌ LEO: self-confident, generous, playful, dramatic, courageous, caring, brave, self-centered
Earth in ♏ SCORPIO: transformative, sexual, secretive, musical, trust-worthy, loyal, supportive, jealous
Sun in ♉ TAURUS: sensual, dependable, resourceful, deliberate, practical, comfortable, stubborn

I take action on

Tarot, Spell, Oracle, Prayer for First Quarter Phase:

Gibbous

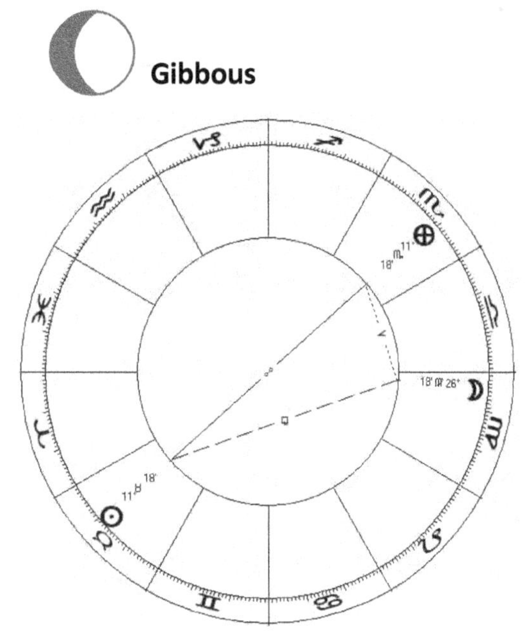

May 1 2023	11:00p	Moon 26°♍18'	Earth 11°♏18'	Sun 11°♉18'
How do I stay on track? What do I need to stay organized? What do I need to compromise? Buds appear and develop in size.				
Moon in ♍ VIRGO: analytical, efficient, healing health-conscious, exacting, technical				
Earth in ♏ SCORPIO: transformative, sexual, secretive, musical, trust-worthy, loyal, supportive, jealous				
Sun in ♉ TAURUS: sensual, dependable, resourceful, deliberate, practical, comfortable, stubborn				

I develop structure with

Tarot, Spell, Oracle, Prayer for Gibbous Phase:

Full-Appulse Lunar Eclipse

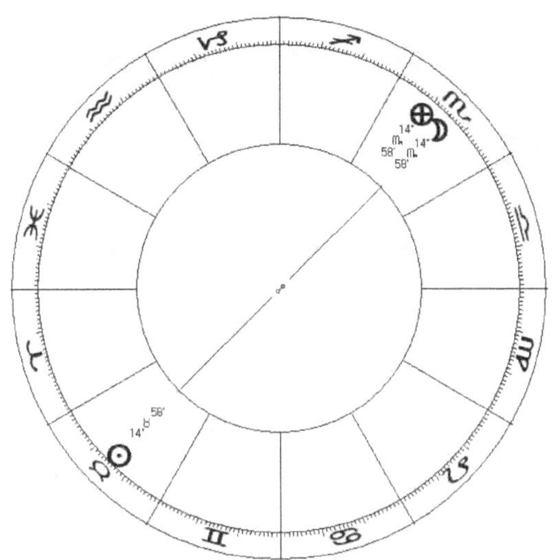

May 5 2023	5:34p	Moon 14°♏58'	Earth 14°♏58'	Sun 14° ♉ 58'

How do function in my world with my process? What does it look like in my day-to-day world? Flower/Fruit
Moon & Earth in ♏ SCORPIO: transformative, sexual, secretive, musical, trust-worthy, loyal, supportive
Sun in ♉ TAURUS: sensual, dependable, resourceful, deliberate, practical, comfortable, stubborn

I communicate my commitment to

Tarot, Spell, Oracle, Prayer for Full Moon Phase:

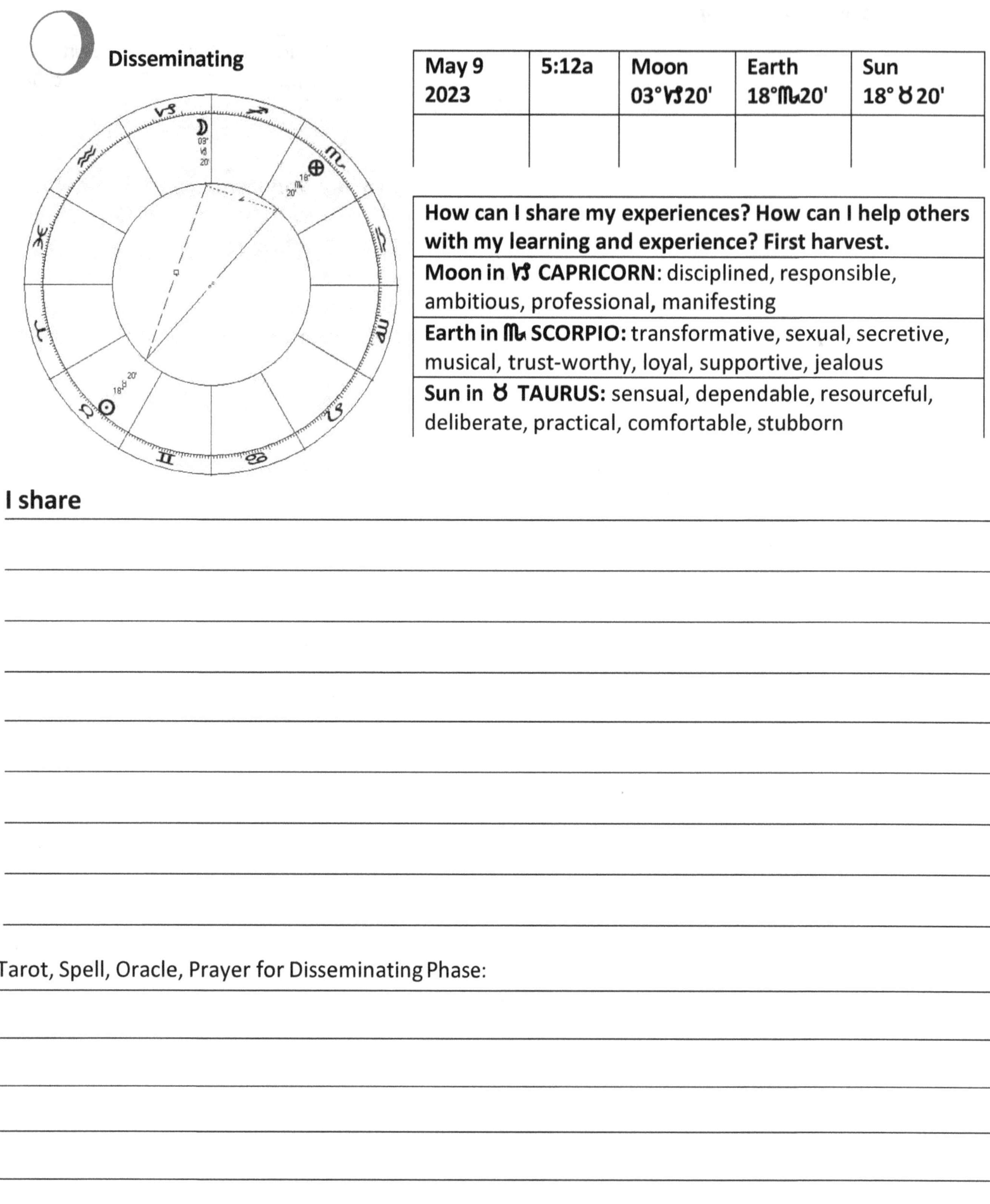

Disseminating

May 9 2023	5:12a	Moon 03°♑20'	Earth 18°♏20'	Sun 18°♉20'

How can I share my experiences? How can I help others with my learning and experience? First harvest.
Moon in ♑ CAPRICORN: disciplined, responsible, ambitious, professional, manifesting
Earth in ♏ SCORPIO: transformative, sexual, secretive, musical, trust-worthy, loyal, supportive, jealous
Sun in ♉ TAURUS: sensual, dependable, resourceful, deliberate, practical, comfortable, stubborn

I share

Tarot, Spell, Oracle, Prayer for Disseminating Phase:

Last Quarter

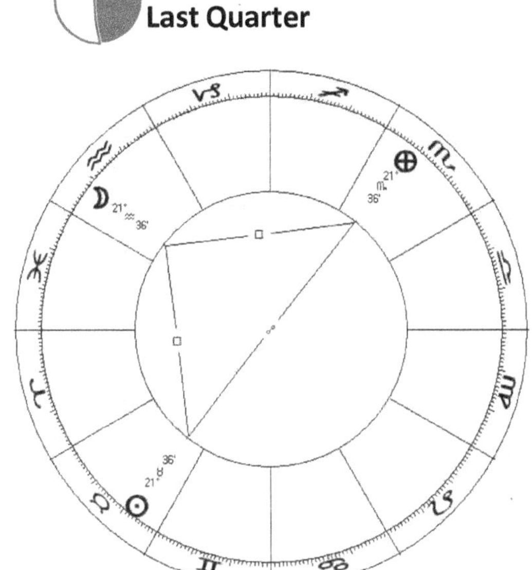

May 12 2023	2:28p	Moon 21°♒36'	Earth 21°♏36'	Sun 21°♉36'

How do I change- let go of the patterns that do not serve me and/or my community? Decay/Last Harvest & composting.
Moon in ♒ AQUARIUS: humanitarian, innovative, progressive, eccentric, detached, friendly
Earth in ♏ SCORPIO: transformative, sexual, secretive, musical, trust-worthy, loyal, supportive, jealous
Sun in ♉ TAURUS: sensual, dependable, resourceful, deliberate, practical, comfortable, stubborn

I change perspective on

Tarot, Spell, Oracle, Prayer for Last Quarter Phase:

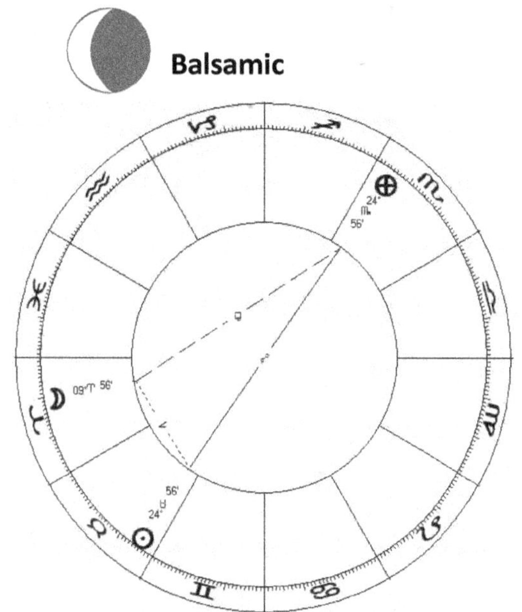

Balsamic

May 16 2023	1:10a	Moon 09°♈56'	Earth 24°♏56'	Sun 24° ♉ 56'

How do I resolve this cycle & visualize, plan? Seed is planted, released to create next cycle/ germination begins.
Moon in ♈ ARIES: assertive, courageous, independent, athletic, enthusiastic, aggressive, initiating
Earth in ♏ SCORPIO: transformative, sexual, secretive, musical, trust-worthy, loyal, supportive, jealous
Sun in ♉ TAURUS: sensual, dependable, resourceful, deliberate, practical, comfortable, stubborn

I resolve/release and/or plan

Tarot, Spell, Oracle, Prayer for Balsamic Phase:

♉ Taurus 2023

Ephemeris at Midnight UTC

Date	Position
May 19 2023	**19°Ta45'**
May 20 2023	**02°Ge48'**
May 21 2023	**15°Ge37'**
May 22 2023	**28°Ge11'**
May 23 2023	**10°Cn32'**
May 24 2023	**22°Cn41'**
May 25 2023	**04°Le41'**
May 26 2023	**16°Le35'**
May 27 2023	**28°Le28'**
May 28 2023	**10°Vi23'**
May 29 2023	**22°Vi26'**
May 30 2023	**04°Li42'**
May 31 2023	**17°Li14'**
Jun 1 2023	**00°Sc08'**
Jun 2 2023	**13°Sc24'**
Jun 3 2023	**27°Sc04'**
Jun 4 2023	**11°Sg06'**
Jun 5 2023	**25°Sg27'**
Jun 6 2023	**10°Cp01'**
Jun 7 2023	**24°Cp41'**
Jun 8 2023	**09°Aq20'**
Jun 9 2023	**23°Aq51'**
Jun 10 2023	**08°Pi11'**
Jun 11 2023	**22°Pi16'**
Jun 12 2023	**06°Ar06'**
Jun 13 2023	**19°Ar41'**
Jun 14 2023	**03°Ta01'**
Jun 15 2023	**16°Ta08'**
Jun 16 2023	**29°Ta03'**
Jun 17 2023	**11°Ge47'**

1st House: my body, my identity, myself, my appearance, my projected image, my soul-purpose, initial approach to life, my interests, my sense of me
2nd House: my talents, my resources, my physical possessions, my money, my personal self-esteem, my sensuous enjoyment, my self-worth
3rd House: my adaptability, my communications, my siblings, my neighborhood, short journey, my active search for knowledge, learning, curiosity, thinking
4th House: my home, family, heritage, my privacy, my emotional life, feelings, eating habits, receptivity, my protective urges, vulnerability
5th House: my creative abilities, my self-expression pregnancy, children, pleasures, will power, romance, merry making, vacation, affection, confidence
6th House: my work conditions & habits, pets, my health, service offered, productivity, training, work skills, hygiene, clothing, nutrition & diet
7th House: agreements, contracts, partnerships, spouse, relationships, consultants, open enemies, receiving love, self-projection, social skills
8th House: loyalty, partner's money & resources, taxes, inheritance, psychic & occult, transformation, shared values, sexual energy, investigations
9th House: wisdom, justice, law, exploration, faith, religious & spiritual, higher education, foreign travel, legal action, experimentation, truth seeking
10th House: accomplishments, authority, recognition, success, reputation, professional affairs, maturity, proficiency, honor, self-fulfillment, public image/life
11th House: groups & clubs, trends, friends, political awareness, emotional detachment, progressive thought, innovative technology & inventions, astrology
12th House: concern for others, self-sacrifice, psychological health, escapism, drug use, pre-natal imprinting, secret keeping, surrender, spirituality

New

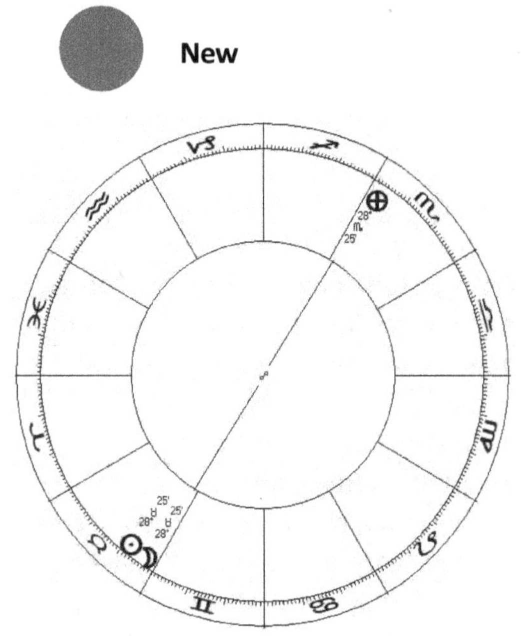

May 19 2023	3:53p	Moon 28° ♉ 25'	Earth 28°♏25'	Sun 28° ♉ 25'

What intuitive sense is emerging within me? Where do I sense my emotions in my body? Germination/Seedling/Germination
Moon & Sun in ♉ TAURUS: sensual, dependable, resourceful, deliberate, practical, comfortable, stubborn
Earth in ♏ SCORPIO: transformative, sexual, secretive, musical, trust-worthy, loyal, supportive, jealous

I emerge with

Tarot, Spell, Oracle, Prayer for New Moon Phase:

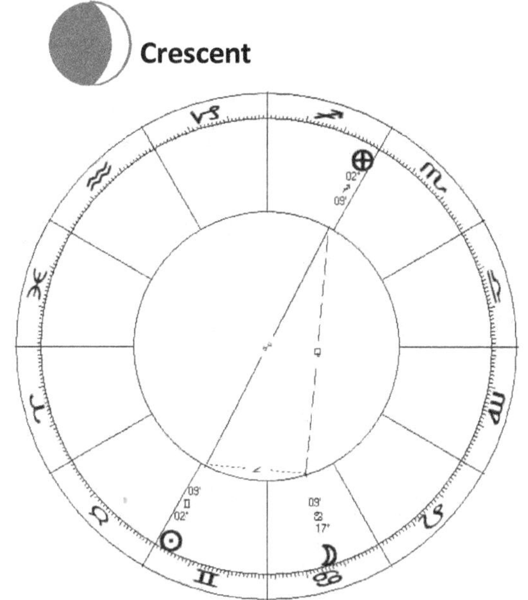

Crescent

May 23 2023	1:01p	Moon 17°♋09'	Earth 02°♐09'	Sun 02°♊09'

What is my challenge? What is my promise? Is my ego an asset or a liability? Sprout
Moon in ♋ CANCER: nurturing, attached, emotional, protective, psychic, domestic, intuitive
Earth in ♐ SAGITTARIUS: philosophical, truth-seeking, ethical, idealistic, optimistic, inspiring, wise, honest
Sun in ♊ GEMINI: Clever, versatile, curious, articulate, adaptable, lighthearted, quick-witted, cheerful

I challenge myself to

Tarot, Spell, Oracle, Prayer for Crescent Phase:

First Quarter

May 27 2023	3:22p	Moon 06°♍05'	Earth 06°♐05'	Sun 06°♊05'

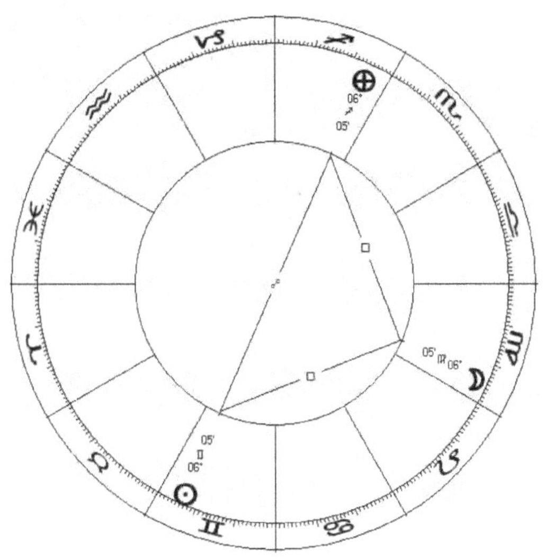

What steps will I take toward accomplishing my goals? How do I move forward? Root/Stem/Leaf - photosynthesis
Moon in ♍ VIRGO: analytical, efficient, healing health-conscious, exacting, technical
Earth in ♐ SAGITTARIUS: philosophical, truth-seeking, ethical, idealistic, optimistic, inspiring, wise, honest
Sun in ♊ GEMINI: Clever, versatile, curious, articulate, adaptable, lighthearted, quick-witted, cheerful

I take action on

Tarot, Spell, Oracle, Prayer for First Quarter Phase:

Gibbous

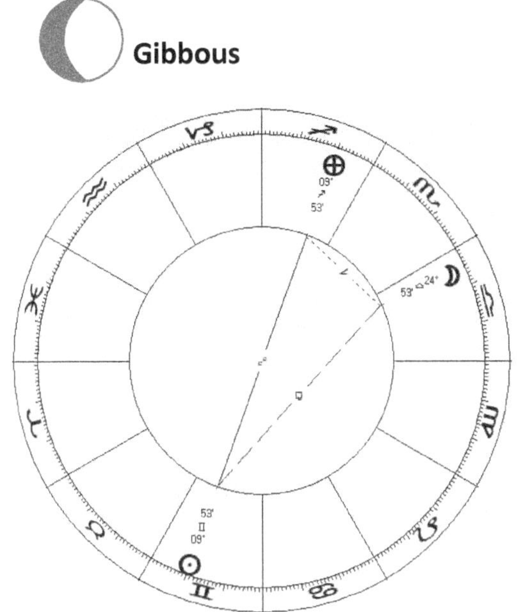

May 31 2023	2:19p	Moon 24°♎53'	Earth 09°♐53'	Sun 09°♊53'

How do I stay on track? What do I need to stay organized? What do I need to compromise? Buds appear and develop in size.
Moon in ♎ LIBRA: cooperative, fair, considerate, artistic, diplomatic, tactful, impartial, refined
Earth in ♐ SAGITTARIUS: philosophical, truth-seeking, ethical, idealistic, optimistic, inspiring, wise, honest
Sun in ♊ GEMINI: Clever, versatile, curious, articulate, adaptable, lighthearted, quick-witted, cheerful

I develop structure with

Tarot, Spell, Oracle, Prayer for Gibbous Phase:

Full

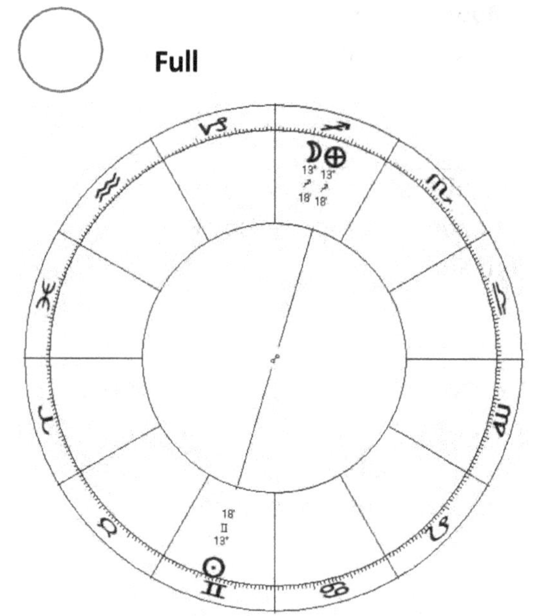

June 4 2023	3:41a	Moon 13°♐18'	Earth 13°♐18'	Sun 13°♊18'

How do function in my world with my process? What does it look like in my day-to-day world? Flower/Fruit
Moon & Earth in ♐ SAGITTARIUS: philosophical, truth-seeking, ethical, idealistic, optimistic, inspiring, wise, honest
Sun in ♊ GEMINI: Clever, versatile, curious, articulate, adaptable, lighthearted, quick-witted, cheerful

I communicate my commitment to

Tarot, Spell, Oracle, Prayer for Full Moon Phase:

Disseminating

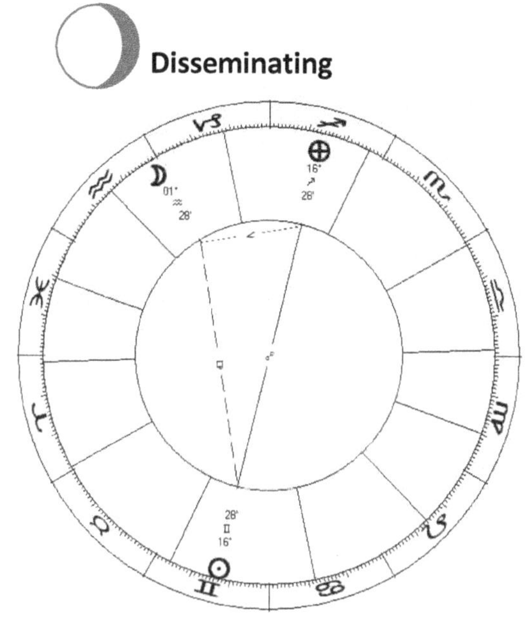

June 7 2023	11:05a	Moon 01°♒28'	Earth 16°♐28'	Sun 16°♊28'

How can I share my experiences? How can I help others with my learning and experience? First harvest.
Moon in ♒ AQUARIUS: humanitarian, innovative, progressive, eccentric, detached, friendly
Earth in ♐ SAGITTARIUS: philosophical, truth-seeking, ethical, idealistic, optimistic, inspiring, wise, honest
Sun in ♊ GEMINI: Clever, versatile, curious, articulate, adaptable, lighthearted, quick-witted, cheerful

I share

Tarot, Spell, Oracle, Prayer for Disseminating Phase:

Last Quarter

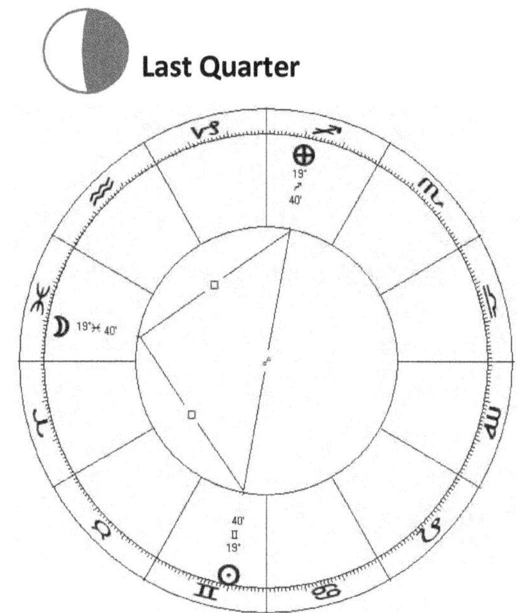

June 10 2023	7:31p	Moon 19°♓40'	Earth 19°♐40'	Sun 19°♊40'

How do I change- let go of the patterns that do not serve me and/or my community? Decay/Last Harvest & composting.
Moon in ♓ PISCES: spiritual, subtle, empathic, psychic, vulnerable, intuitive, self- sacrificing, artistic
Earth in ♐ SAGITTARIUS: philosophical, truth-seeking, ethical, idealistic, optimistic, inspiring, wise, honest
Sun in ♊ GEMINI: Clever, versatile, curious, articulate, adaptable, lighthearted, quick-witted, cheerful

I change perspective on

Tarot, Spell, Oracle, Prayer for Last Quarter Phase:

Balsamic

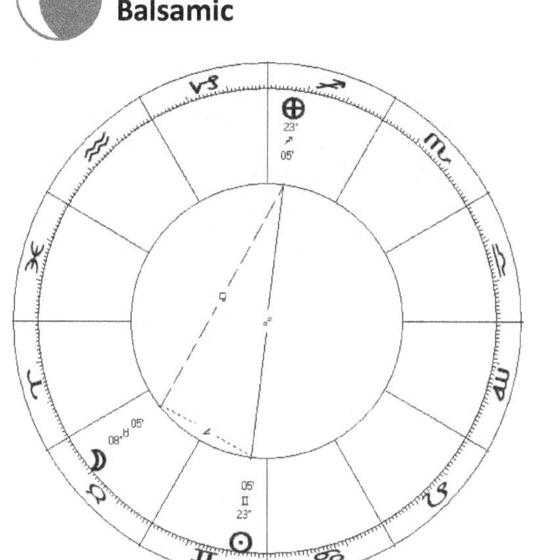

June 14 2023	9:12a	Moon 08° ♉ 05'	Earth 23° ♐ 05'	Sun 23° ♊ 05'

How do I resolve this cycle & visualize, plan? Seed is planted, released to create next cycle/ germination begins.
Moon in ♉ TAURUS: sensual, dependable, resourceful, deliberate, practical, comfortable, stubborn
Earth in ♐ SAGITTARIUS: philosophical, truth-seeking, ethical, idealistic, optimistic, inspiring, wise, honest
Sun in ♊ GEMINI: Clever, versatile, curious, articulate, adaptable, lighthearted, quick-witted, cheerful

I resolve/release and/or plan

Tarot, Spell, Oracle, Prayer for Balsamic Phase:

Ⅱ Gemini 2023

Ephemeris at Mi	dnight UTC
Jun 18 2023	24°Ge19'
Jun 19 2023	06°Cn41'
Jun 20 2023	18°Cn54'
Jun 21 2023	00°Le57'
Jun 22 2023	12°Le54'
Jun 23 2023	24°Le46'
Jun 24 2023	06°Vi37'
Jun 25 2023	18°Vi30'
Jun 26 2023	00°Li31'
Jun 27 2023	12°Li44'
Jun 28 2023	25°Li15'
Jun 29 2023	08°Sc08'
Jun 30 2023	21°Sc26'
Jul 1 2023	05°Sg13'
Jul 2 2023	19°Sg27'
Jul 3 2023	04°Cp05'
Jul 4 2023	19°Cp01'
Jul 5 2023	04°Aq05'
Jul 6 2023	19°Aq07'
Jul 7 2023	03°Pi58'
Jul 8 2023	18°Pi32'
Jul 9 2023	02°Ar44'
Jul 10 2023	16°Ar34'
Jul 11 2023	00°Ta02'
Jul 12 2023	13°Ta11'
Jul 13 2023	26°Ta03'
Jul 14 2023	08°Ge42'
Jul 15 2023	21°Ge09'
Jul 16 2023	03°Cn27'

1st House: my body, my identity, myself, my appearance, my projected image, my soul-purpose, initial approach to life, my interests, my sense of me
2nd House: my talents, my resources, my physical possessions, my money, my personal self-esteem, my sensuous enjoyment, my self-worth
3rd House: my adaptability, my communications, my siblings, my neighborhood, short journey, my active search for knowledge, learning, curiosity, thinking
4th House: my home, family, heritage, my privacy, my emotional life, feelings, eating habits, receptivity, my protective urges, vulnerability
5th House: my creative abilities, my self-expression pregnancy, children, pleasures, will power, romance, merry making, vacation, affection, confidence
6th House: my work conditions & habits, pets, my health, service offered, productivity, training, work skills, hygiene, clothing, nutrition & diet
7th House: agreements, contracts, partnerships, spouse, relationships, consultants, open enemies, receiving love, self-projection, social skills
8th House: loyalty, partner's money & resources, taxes, inheritance, psychic & occult, transformation, shared values, sexual energy, investigations
9th House: wisdom, justice, law, exploration, faith, religious & spiritual, higher education, foreign travel, legal action, experimentation, truth seeking
10th House: accomplishments, authority, recognition, success, reputation, professional affairs, maturity, proficiency, honor, self-fulfillment, public image/life
11th House: groups & clubs, trends, friends, political awareness, emotional detachment, progressive thought, innovative technology & inventions, astrology
12th House: concern for others, self-sacrifice, psychological health, escapism, drug use, pre-natal imprinting, secret keeping, surrender, spirituality

New

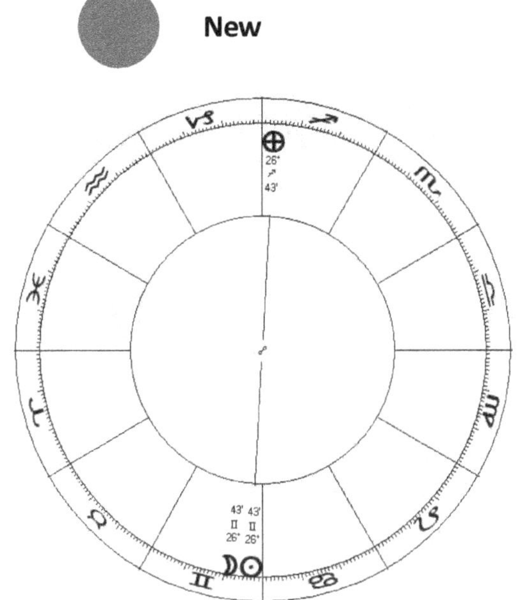

June 18 2023	4:37a	Moon 26°♊43'	Earth 26°♐43'	Sun 26°♊43'

What intuitive sense is emerging within me? Where do I sense my emotions in my body? Germination/Seedling/Germination
Moon & Sun in ♊ GEMINI: Clever, versatile, curious, articulate, adaptable, lighthearted, quick-witted, cheerful
Earth in ♐SAGITTARIUS: philosophical, truth-seeking, ethical, idealistic, optimistic, inspiring, wise, honest

I emerge with

Tarot, Spell, Oracle, Prayer for New Moon Phase:

Crescent

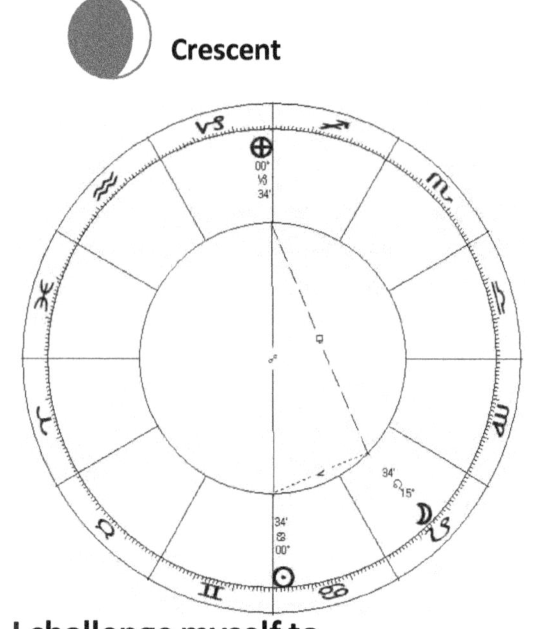

June 22 2023	5:22a	Moon 15°♌34'	Earth 00°♑34'	Sun 00°♋34'

What is my challenge? What is my promise? Is my ego an asset or liability? Sprout
Moon in ♌ LEO: self-confident, generous, playful, dramatic, courageous, caring, brave, self-centered
Earth in ♑ CAPRICORN: disciplined, responsible, ambitious, professional, manifesting
Sun in ♋ CANCER: nurturing, attached, emotional, protective, psychic, domestic, intuitive

I challenge myself to

Tarot, Spell, Oracle, Prayer for Crescent Phase:

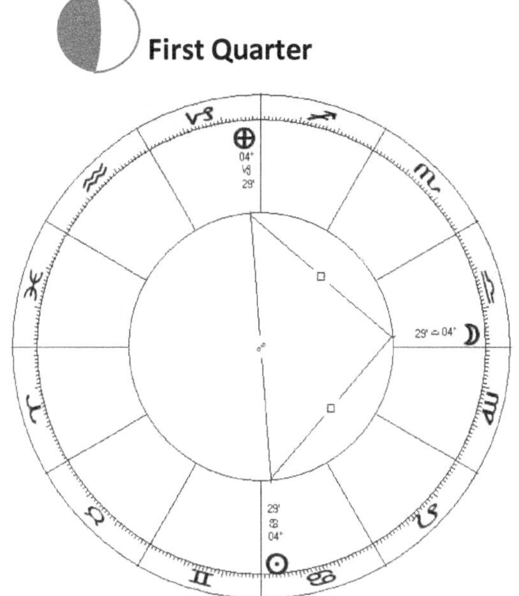

First Quarter

June 26 2023	7:49a	Moon 04°♎29'	Earth 04°♑29'	Sun 04°♋29'

What steps will I take toward accomplishing my goals? How do I move forward? Root/Stem/Leaf - photosynthesis
Moon in ♎ LIBRA: cooperative, fair, considerate, artistic, diplomatic, tactful, impartial, refined
Earth in ♑CAPRICORN: disciplined, responsible, ambitious, professional, manifesting
Sun in ♋ CANCER: nurturing, attached, emotional, protective, psychic, domestic, intuitive

I take action on

Tarot, Spell, Oracle, Prayer for First Quarter Phase:

Gibbous

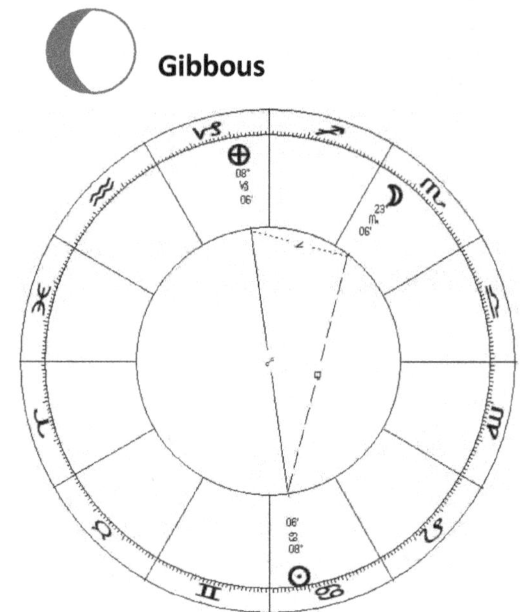

June 30 2023	2:55a	Moon 23°♏06'	Earth 08°♑06'	Sun 08°♋06'

How do I stay on track? What do I need to stay organized? What do I need to compromise? Buds appear and develop in size.
Moon in ♏ SCORPIO: transformative, sexual, secretive, musical, trust-worthy, loyal, supportive, jealous
Earth in ♑ CAPRICORN: disciplined, responsible, ambitious, professional, manifesting
Sun in ♋ CANCER: nurturing, attached, emotional, protective, psychic, domestic, intuitive

I develop structure with

Tarot, Spell, Oracle, Prayer for Gibbous Phase:

Full

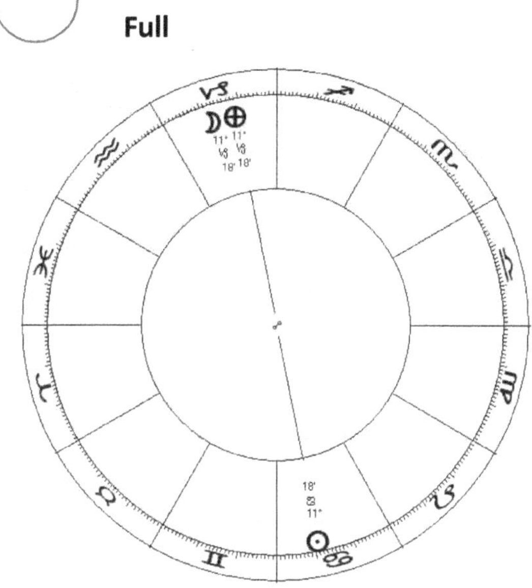

July 3 2023	11:38a	Moon 11°♑18'	Earth 11°♑18'	Sun 11°♋18'

How do function in my world with my process? What does it look like in my day-to-day world? Flower/Fruit
Moon & Earth in ♑CAPRICORN: disciplined, responsible, ambitious, professional, manifesting
Sun in ♋ CANCER: nurturing, attached, emotional, protective, psychic, domestic, intuitive

I communicate my commitment to

Tarot, Spell, Oracle, Prayer for Full Moon Phase:

Disseminating

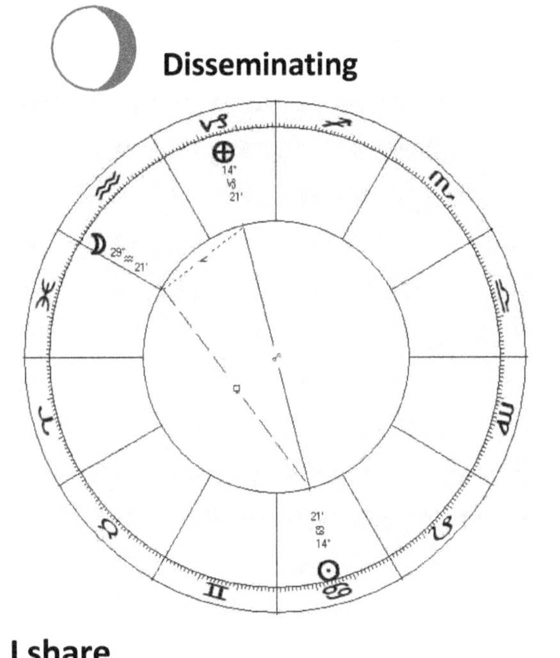

July 6 2023	4:30p	Moon 29°♒21'	Earth 14°♑21'	Sun 14°♋21'

How can I share my experiences? How can I help others with my learning and experience? First harvest.
Moon in ♒ AQUARIUS: humanitarian, innovative, progressive, eccentric, detached, friendly
Earth in ♑ CAPRICORN: disciplined, responsible, ambitious, professional, manifesting
Sun in ♋ CANCER: nurturing, attached, emotional, protective, psychic, domestic, intuitive

I share

Tarot, Spell, Oracle, Prayer for Disseminating Phase:

Last Quarter

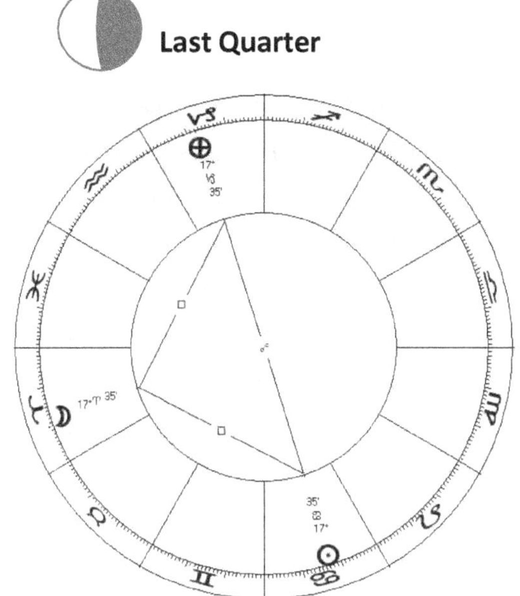

July 10 2023	1:47a	Moon 17°♈35'	Earth 17°♑35'	Sun 17°♋35'

How do I change- let go of the patterns that do not serve me and/or my community? Decay/Last Harvest & composting.
Moon in ♈ ARIES: assertive, courageous, independent, athletic, enthusiastic, aggressive, initiating
Earth in ♑CAPRICORN: disciplined, responsible, ambitious, professional, manifesting
Sun in ♋ CANCER: nurturing, attached, emotional, protective, psychic, domestic, intuitive

I change perspective on

Tarot, Spell, Oracle, Prayer for Last Quarter Phase:

Balsamic

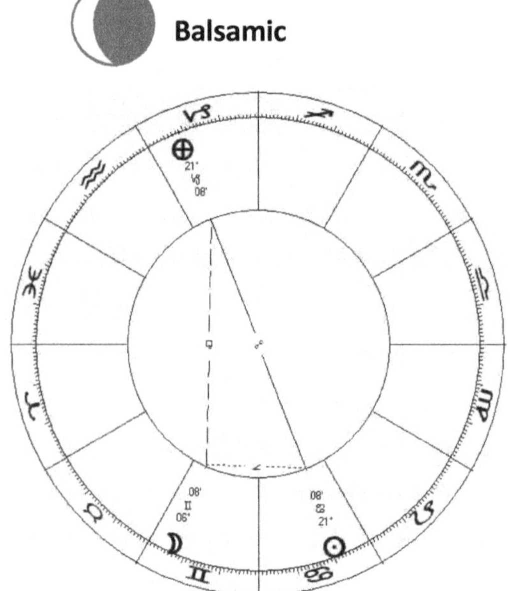

July 13 2023	7:06p	Moon 06° ♊ 08'	Earth 21° ♑ 08'	Sun 21° ♋ 08'
How do I resolve this cycle & visualize, and plan? Seed is planted, released to create the next cycle/ germination begins.				
Moon in ♊ GEMINI: Clever, versatile, curious, articulate, adaptable, lighthearted, quick-witted, cheerful				
Earth in ♑ CAPRICORN: disciplined, responsible, ambitious, professional, manifesting				
Sun in ♋ CANCER: nurturing, attached, emotional, protective, psychic, domestic, intuitive				

I resolve/release and/or plan

Tarot, Spell, Oracle, Prayer for Balsamic Phase:

♋ Cancer 2023

Ephemeris at Midnight UTC

Jul 17 2023	15°Cn37'
Jul 18 2023	27°Cn40'
Jul 19 2023	09°Le37'
Jul 20 2023	21°Le30'
Jul 21 2023	03°Vi20'
Jul 22 2023	15°Vi10'
Jul 23 2023	27°Vi03'
Jul 24 2023	09°Li03'
Jul 25 2023	21°Li14'
Jul 26 2023	03°Sc42'
Jul 27 2023	16°Sc31'
Jul 28 2023	29°Sc46'
Jul 29 2023	13°Sg30'
Jul 30 2023	27°Sg44'
Jul 31 2023	12°Cp26'
Aug 1 2023	27°Cp29'
Aug 2 2023	12°Aq45'
Aug 3 2023	28°Aq02'
Aug 4 2023	13°Pi09'
Aug 5 2023	27°Pi58'
Aug 6 2023	12°Ar23'
Aug 7 2023	26°Ar20'
Aug 8 2023	09°Ta52'
Aug 9 2023	22°Ta59'
Aug 10 2023	05°Ge46'
Aug 11 2023	18°Ge17'
Aug 12 2023	00°Cn34'
Aug 13 2023	12°Cn42'
Aug 14 2023	24°Cn43'
Aug 15 2023	06°Le39'

1st House: my body, my identity, myself, my appearance, my projected image, my soul-purpose, initial approach to life, my interests, my sense of me
2nd House: my talents, my resources, my physical possessions, my money, my personal self-esteem, my sensuous enjoyment, my self-worth
3rd House: my adaptability, my communications, my siblings, my neighborhood, short journey, my active search for knowledge, learning, curiosity, thinking
4th House: my home, family, heritage, my privacy, my emotional life, feelings, eating habits, receptivity, my protective urges, vulnerability
5th House: my creative abilities, my self-expression pregnancy, children, pleasures, will power, romance, merry making, vacation, affection, confidence
6th House: my work conditions & habits, pets, my health, service offered, productivity, training, work skills, hygiene, clothing, nutrition & diet
7th House: agreements, contracts, partnerships, spouse, relationships, consultants, open enemies, receiving love, self-projection, social skills
8th House: loyalty, partner's money & resources, taxes, inheritance, psychic & occult, transformation, shared values, sexual energy, investigations
9th House: wisdom, justice, law, exploration, faith, religious & spiritual, higher education, foreign travel, legal action, experimentation, truth seeking
10th House: accomplishments, authority, recognition, success, reputation, professional affairs, maturity, proficiency, honor, self-fulfillment, public image/life
11th House: groups & clubs, trends, friends, political awareness, emotional detachment, progressive thought, innovative technology & inventions, astrology
12th House: concern for others, self-sacrifice, psychological health, escapism, drug use, pre-natal imprinting, secret keeping, surrender, spirituality

New Moon

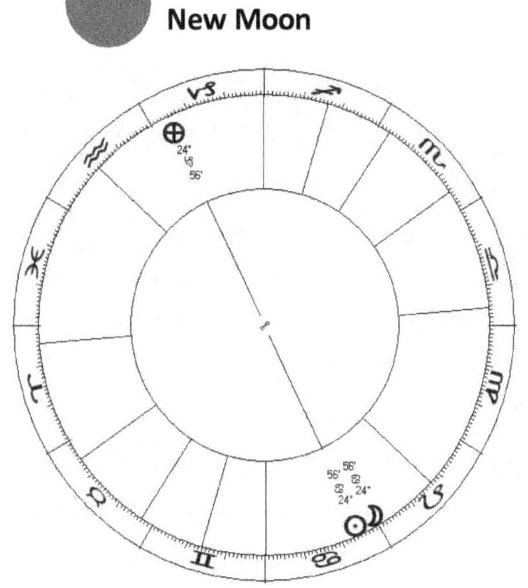

July 17 2023	6:31p	Moon 24°♋56'	Earth 24°♑56'	Sun 24°♋56'

What intuitive sense is emerging within me? Where do I sense my emotions in my body? Germination/Seedling/Germination
Moon & Sun in ♋ CANCER: nurturing, attached, emotional, protective, psychic, domestic, intuitive
Earth in ♑CAPRICORN: disciplined, responsible, ambitious, professional, manifesting

I emerge with

Tarot, Spell, Oracle, Prayer for New Moon Phase:

Crescent

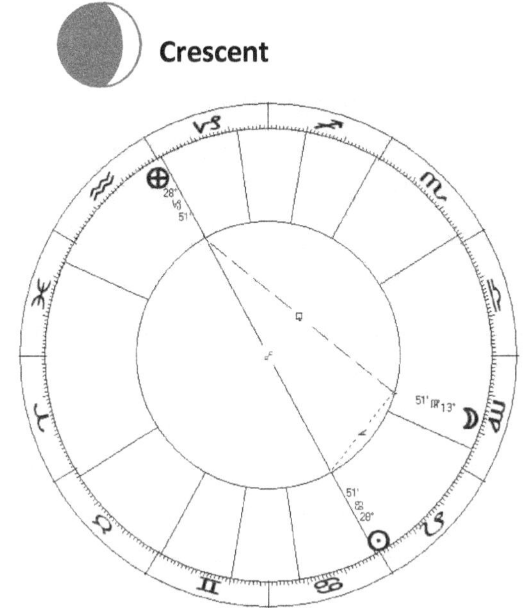

July 21 2023	9:20p	Moon 13°♍51'	Earth 28°♑51'	Sun 28°♋51'

What is my challenge? What is my promise? Is my ego an asset or liability? Sprout
Moon in ♍ VIRGO: analytical, efficient, healing health-conscious, exacting, technical
Sun in ♋ CANCER: nurturing, attached, emotional, protective, psychic, domestic, intuitive
Earth in ♑CAPRICORN: disciplined, responsible, ambitious, professional, manifesting

I challenge myself to

Tarot, Spell, Oracle, Prayer for Crescent Phase:

First Quarter

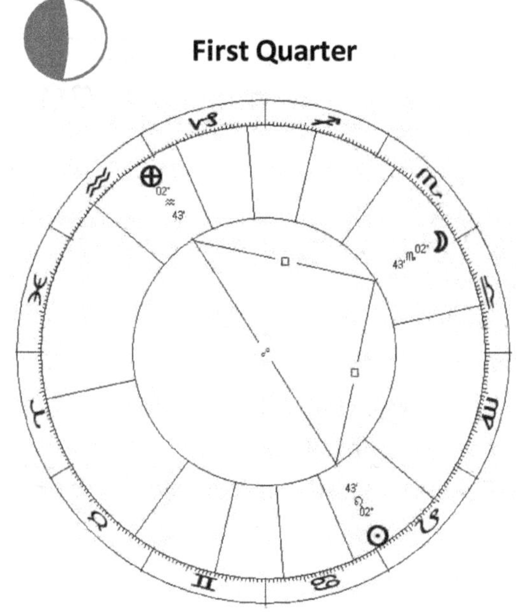

July 25 2023	10:06p	Moon 02°♏43'	Earth 02°♒43'	Sun 02°♌43'

What steps will I take toward accomplishing my goals? How do I move forward? Root/Stem/Leaf - photosynthesis
Moon in ♏ SCORPIO: transformative, sexual, secretive, musical, trust-worthy, loyal, supportive, jealous
Earth in ♒ AQUARIUS: humanitarian, innovative, progressive, eccentric, detached, friendly
Sun in ♌ LEO: self-confident, generous, playful, dramatic, courageous, caring, brave, self-centered

I take action on

Tarot, Spell, Oracle, Prayer for First Quarter Phase:

Gibbous

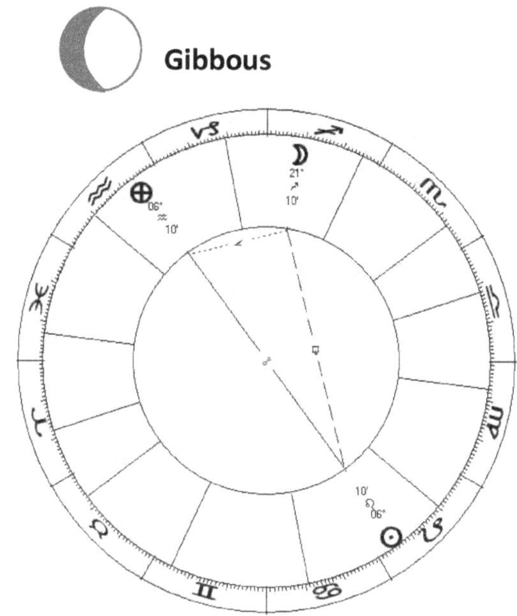

July 29 2023	1:01p	Moon 21°♐10'	Earth 06°♒10'	Sun 06°♌10'

How do I stay on track? What do I need to stay organized? What do I need to compromise? Buds appear and develop in size.
Moon in ♐ SAGITTARIUS: philosophical, truth-seeking, ethical, idealistic, optimistic, inspiring, wise, honest
Earth in ♒ AQUARIUS: humanitarian, innovative, progressive, eccentric, detached, friendly
Sun in ♌ LEO: self-confident, generous, playful, dramatic, courageous, caring, brave, self-centered

I develop structure with

Tarot, Spell, Oracle, Prayer for Gibbous Phase:

Full

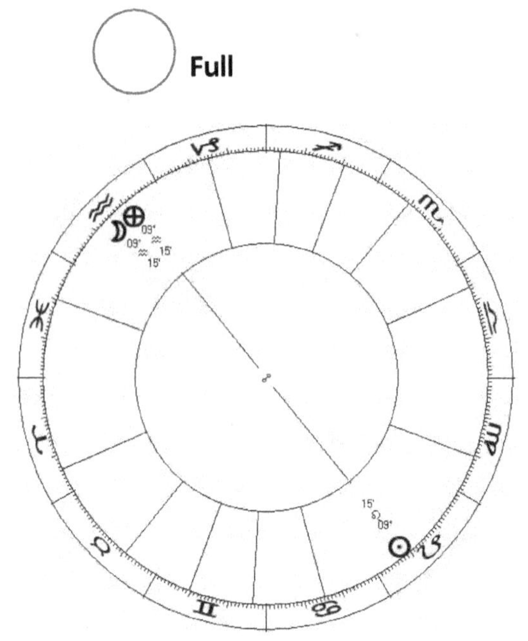

Aug 1 2023	6:31p	Moon 09°♒15'	Earth 09°♒15'	Sun 09°♌15'

How do function in my world with my process? What does it look like in my day-to-day world? Flower/Fruit
Moon & Moon in ♒ AQUARIUS: humanitarian, innovative, progressive, eccentric, detached, friendly
Sun in ♌ LEO: self-confident, generous, playful, dramatic, courageous, caring, brave, self-centered

I communicate my commitment to

Tarot, Spell, Oracle, Prayer for Full Moon Phase:

Disseminating

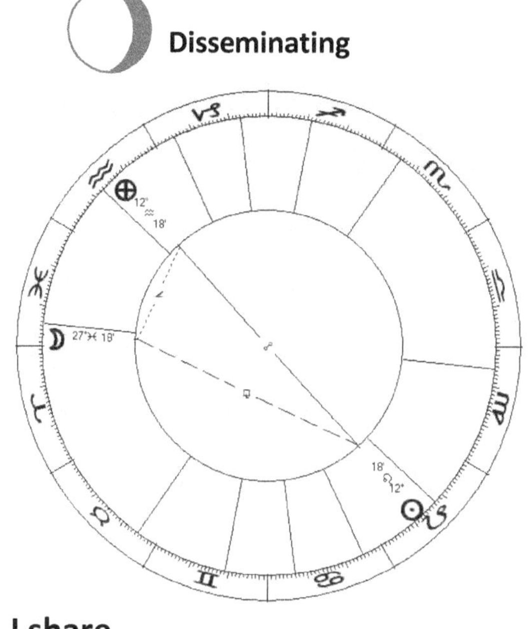

Aug 4 2023	10:53p	Moon 27°♓18'	Earth 12°♒18'	Sun 12°♌18'

How can I share my experiences? How can I help others with my learning and experience? First harvest.
Moon in ♓ PISCES: spiritual, subtle, empathic, psychic, vulnerable, intuitive, self- sacrificing, artistic
Earth in ♒ AQUARIUS: humanitarian, innovative, progressive, eccentric, detached, friendly
Sun in ♌ LEO: self-confident, generous, playful, dramatic, courageous, caring, brave, self-centered

I share

Tarot, Spell, Oracle, Prayer for Disseminating Phase:

Last Quarter

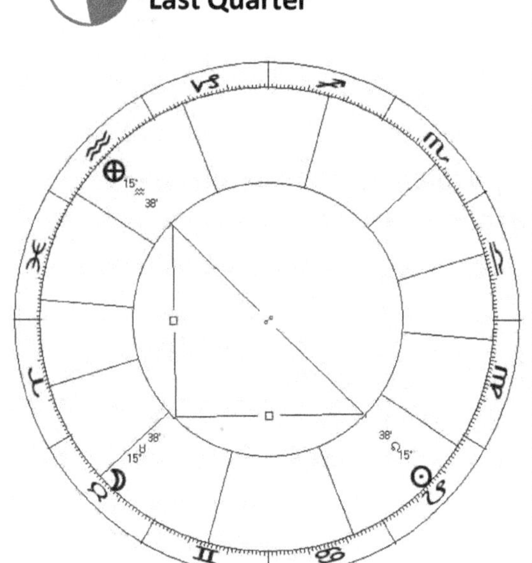

Aug 8 2023	10:28a	Moon 15° ♉ 38'	Earth 15° ♒ 38'	Sun 15° ♌ 38'

How do I change- let go of the patterns that do not serve me and/or my community? Decay/Last Harvest & composting.
Moon in ♉ TAURUS: sensual, dependable, resourceful, deliberate, practical, comfortable, stubborn
Earth in ♒ AQUARIUS: humanitarian, innovative, progressive, eccentric, detached, friendly
Sun in ♌ LEO: self-confident, generous, playful, dramatic, courageous, caring, brave, self-centered

I change perspective on

Tarot, Spell, Oracle, Prayer for Last Quarter Phase:

Balsamic

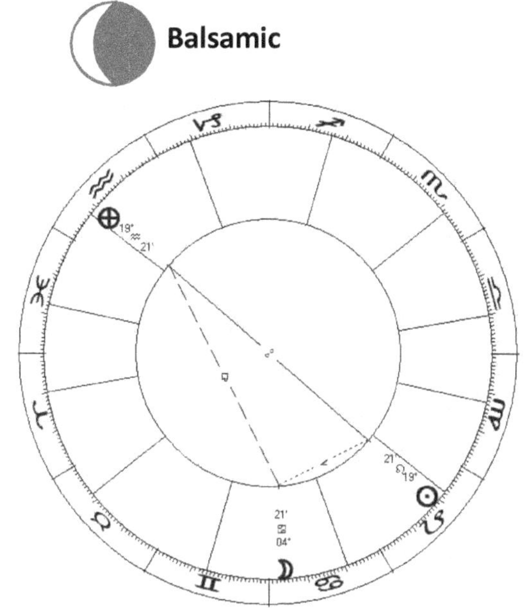

Aug 12 2023	7:27a	Moon 04°♋21'	Earth 19°♒21'	Sun 19°♌21'

How do I resolve this cycle & visualize, plan? Seed is planted, released to create next cycle/ germination begins.
Moon in ♋ CANCER: nurturing, attached, emotional, protective, psychic, domestic, intuitive
Earth in ♒ AQUARIUS: humanitarian, innovative, progressive, eccentric, detached, friendly
Sun in ♌ LEO: self-confident, generous, playful, dramatic, courageous, caring, brave, self-centered

I resolve/release and/or plan

Tarot, Spell, Oracle, Prayer for Balsamic Phase:

♌ Leo 2023

Ephemeris at Midnight UTC	
Aug 16 2023	18°Le31'
Aug 17 2023	00°Vi22'
Aug 18 2023	12°Vi13'
Aug 19 2023	24°Vi05'
Aug 20 2023	06°Li02'
Aug 21 2023	18°Li05'
Aug 22 2023	00°Sc19'
Aug 23 2023	12°Sc47'
Aug 24 2023	25°Sc35'
Aug 25 2023	08°Sg45'
Aug 26 2023	22°Sg22'
Aug 27 2023	06°Cp27'
Aug 28 2023	21°Cp00'
Aug 29 2023	05°Aq55'
Aug 30 2023	21°Aq07'
Aug 31 2023	06°Pi24'
Sep 1 2023	21°Pi36'
Sep 2 2023	06°Ar33'
Sep 3 2023	21°Ar07'
Sep 4 2023	05°Ta14'
Sep 5 2023	18°Ta54'
Sep 6 2023	02°Ge06'
Sep 7 2023	14°Ge56'
Sep 8 2023	27°Ge25'
Sep 9 2023	09°Cn40'
Sep 10 2023	21°Cn44'
Sep 11 2023	03°Le40'
Sep 12 2023	15°Le32'
Sep 13 2023	27°Le22'
Sep 14 2023	09°Vi14'

1st House: my body, my identity, myself, my appearance, my projected image, my soul-purpose, initial approach to life, my interests, my sense of me
2nd House: my talents, my resources, my physical possessions, my money, my personal self-esteem, my sensuous enjoyment, my self-worth
3rd House: my adaptability, my communications, my siblings, my neighborhood, short journey, my active search for knowledge, learning, curiosity, thinking
4th House: my home, family, heritage, my privacy, my emotional life, feelings, eating habits, receptivity, my protective urges, vulnerability
5th House: my creative abilities, my self-expression pregnancy, children, pleasures, will power, romance, merry making, vacation, affection, confidence
6th House: my work conditions & habits, pets, my health, service offered, productivity, training, work skills, hygiene, clothing, nutrition & diet
7th House: agreements, contracts, partnerships, spouse, relationships, consultants, open enemies, receiving love, self-projection, social skills
8th House: loyalty, partner's money & resources, taxes, inheritance, psychic & occult, transformation, shared values, sexual energy, investigations
9th House: wisdom, justice, law, exploration, faith, religious & spiritual, higher education, foreign travel, legal action, experimentation, truth seeking
10th House: accomplishments, authority, recognition, success, reputation, professional affairs, maturity, proficiency, honor, self-fulfillment, public image/life
11th House: groups & clubs, trends, friends, political awareness, emotional detachment, progressive thought, innovative technology & inventions, astrology
12th House: concern for others, self-sacrifice, psychological health, escapism, drug use, pre-natal imprinting, secret keeping, surrender, spirituality

New

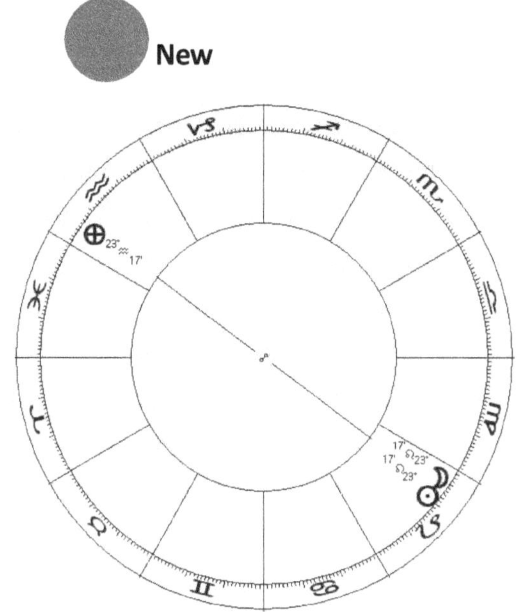

Aug 16 2023	9:38a	Moon 23°♌17'	Earth 23°♒17'	Sun 23°♌17'

What intuitive sense is emerging within me? Where do I sense my emotions in my body? Germination/Seedling/Germination
Moon & Sun in ♌ LEO: self-confident, generous, playful, dramatic, courageous, caring, brave, self-centered
Earth in ♒ AQUARIUS: humanitarian, innovative, progressive, eccentric, detached, friendly

I emerge with

Tarot, Spell, Oracle, Prayer for New Moon Phase:

Crescent

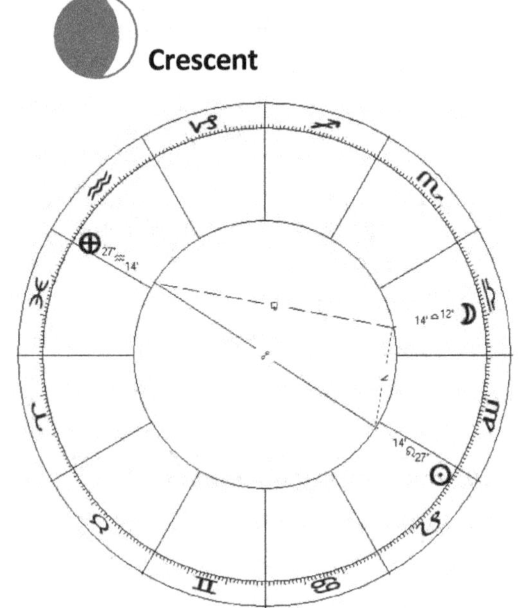

Aug 20 2023	12:23p	Moon 12°♎14'	Earth 27°♒14'	Sun 27°♌14'

What is my challenge? What is my promise? Is my ego an asset or a liability? Sprout
Moon in ♎ LIBRA: cooperative, fair, considerate, artistic, diplomatic, tactful, impartial, refined
Earth in ♒AQUARIUS: humanitarian, innovative, progressive, eccentric, detached, friendly
Sun in ♌ LEO: self-confident, generous, playful, dramatic, courageous, caring, brave, self-centered

I challenge myself to

Tarot, Spell, Oracle, Prayer for Crescent Phase:

First Quarter

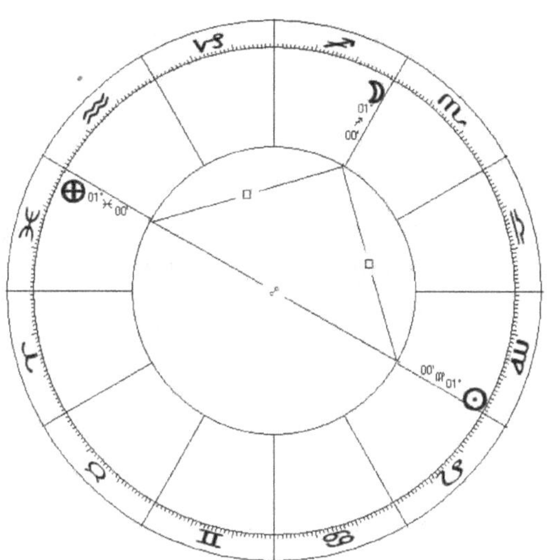

Aug 24 2023	9:57a	Moon 01°♐00'	Earth 01°♓00'	Sun 01°♍00'

What steps will I take toward accomplishing my goals? How do I move forward? Root/Stem/Leaf - photosynthesis
Moon in ♐ SAGITTARIUS: philosophical, truth-seeking, ethical, idealistic, optimistic, inspiring, wise, honest
Earth in ♓ PISCES: spiritual, subtle, empathic, psychic, vulnerable, intuitive, self-sacrificing, artistic
Sun in ♍ VIRGO: analytical, efficient, healing health-conscious, exacting, technical

I take action on

Tarot, Spell, Oracle, Prayer for First Quarter Phase:

Gibbous

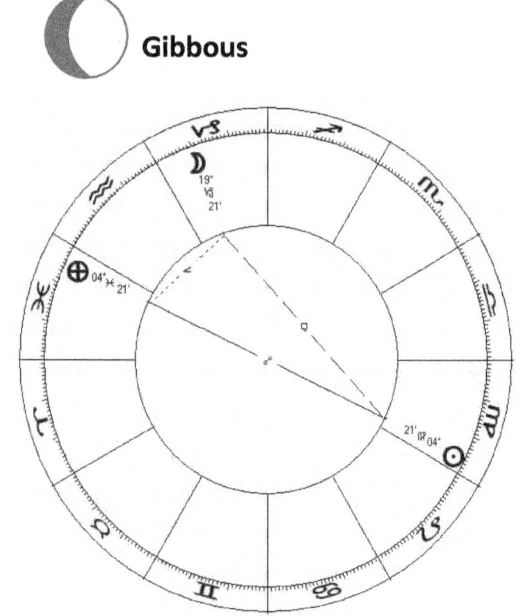

Aug 27 2023	9:18p	Moon 19°♑21'	Earth 04°♓21'	Sun 04°♍21'

How do I stay on track? What do I need to stay organized? What do I need to compromise? Buds appear and develop in size.
Moon in ♑CAPRICORN: disciplined, responsible, ambitious, professional, manifesting
Earth in ♓ PISCES: spiritual, subtle, empathic, psychic, vulnerable, intuitive, self- sacrificing, artistic
Sun in ♍ VIRGO: analytical, efficient, healing health-conscious, exacting, technical

I develop structure with

Tarot, Spell, Oracle, Prayer for Gibbous Phase:

Full

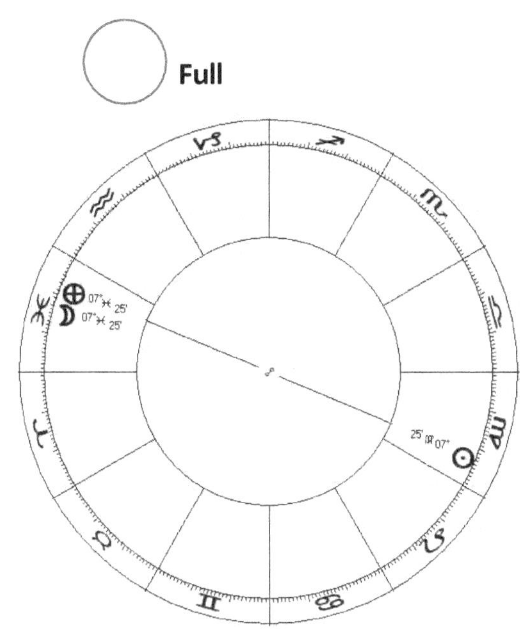

Aug 31 2023	1:35a	Moon 07°♓25'	Earth 07°♓25'	Sun 07°♍25'

How do function in my world with my process? What does it look like in my day-to-day world? Flower/Fruit
Moon in ♓ PISCES: spiritual, subtle, empathic, psychic, vulnerable, intuitive, self- sacrificing, artistic
Earth in ♓ PISCES: spiritual, subtle, empathic, psychic, vulnerable, intuitive, self- sacrificing, artistic
Sun in ♍ VIRGO: analytical, efficient, healing health-conscious, exacting, technical

I communicate my commitment to

Tarot, Spell, Oracle, Prayer for Full Moon Phase:

Disseminating

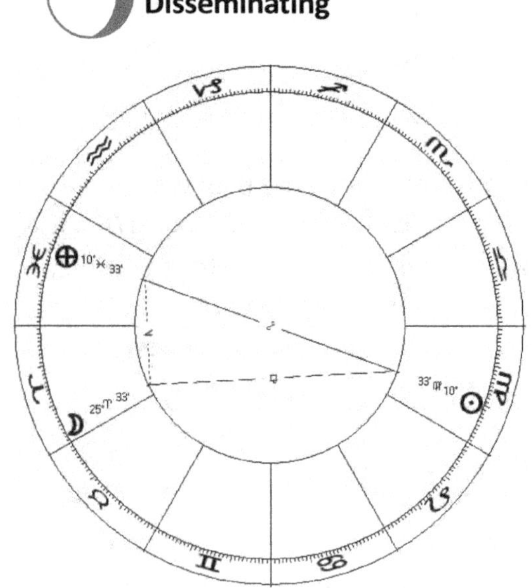

Sep 3 2023	7:27a	Moon 25°♈33'	Earth 10°♓33'	Sun 10°♍33'

How can I share my experiences? How can I help others with my learning and experience? First harvest.
Moon in ♈ ARIES: assertive, courageous, independent, athletic, enthusiastic, aggressive, initiating
Earth in ♓ PISCES: spiritual, subtle, empathic, psychic, vulnerable, intuitive, self- sacrificing, artistic
Sun in ♍ VIRGO: analytical, efficient, healing health-conscious, exacting, technical

I share

Tarot, Spell, Oracle, Prayer for Disseminating Phase:

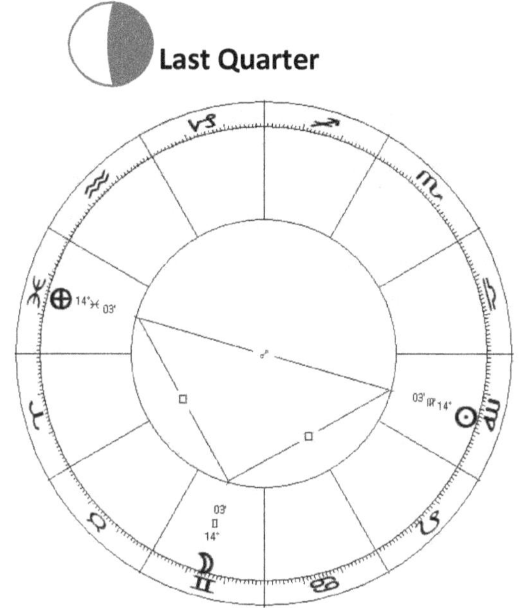

Sep 6 2023	10:21p	Moon 14° ♊ 03'	Earth 14° ♓ 03'	Sun 14° ♍ 03'

How do I change- let go of the patterns that do not serve me and/or my community?
Decay/Last Harvest & composting.

Moon in ♊ GEMINI: Clever, versatile, curious, articulate, adaptable, lighthearted, quick-witted, cheerful

Earth in ♓ PISCES: spiritual, subtle, empathic, psychic, vulnerable, intuitive, self- sacrificing, artistic

Sun in ♍ VIRGO: analytical, efficient, healing health-conscious, exacting, technical

I change perspective on

Tarot, Spell, Oracle, Prayer for Last Quarter Phase:

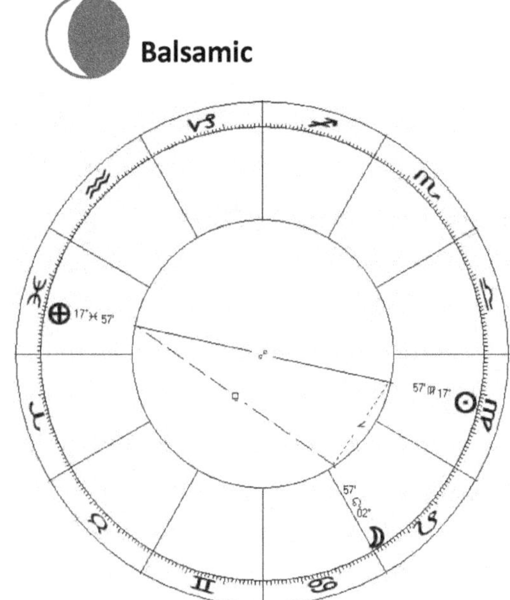

Sep 10 2023	10:34p	Moon 02°♌57'	Earth 17°♓57'	Sun 17°♍57'

How do I resolve this cycle & visualize, plan? Seed is planted, released to create next cycle/ germination begins.
Moon in ♌ LEO: self-confident, generous, playful, dramatic, courageous, caring, brave, self-centered
Earth in ♓ PISCES: spiritual, subtle, empathic, psychic, vulnerable, intuitive, self- sacrificing, artistic
Sun in ♍ VIRGO: analytical, efficient, healing health-conscious, exacting, technical

I resolve/release and/or plan

Tarot, Spell, Oracle, Prayer for Balsamic Phase:

♍ Virgo 2023

Ephemeris at Midnight UTC	
Sep 15 2023	21°Vi09'
Sep 16 2023	03°Li08'
Sep 17 2023	15°Li13'
Sep 18 2023	27°Li26'
Sep 19 2023	09°Sc50'
Sep 20 2023	22°Sc28'
Sep 21 2023	05°Sg20'
Sep 22 2023	18°Sg32'
Sep 23 2023	02°Cp05'
Sep 24 2023	16°Cp00'
Sep 25 2023	00°Aq18'
Sep 26 2023	14°Aq56'
Sep 27 2023	29°Aq48'
Sep 28 2023	14°Pi49'
Sep 29 2023	29°Pi49'
Sep 30 2023	14°Ar39'
Oct 1 2023	29°Ar13'
Oct 2 2023	13°Ta24'
Oct 3 2023	27°Ta09'
Oct 4 2023	10°Ge29'
Oct 5 2023	23°Ge24'
Oct 6 2023	05°Cn57'
Oct 7 2023	18°Cn14'
Oct 8 2023	00°Le17'
Oct 9 2023	12°Le12'
Oct 10 2023	24°Le03'
Oct 11 2023	05°Vi54'
Oct 12 2023	17°Vi48'
Oct 13 2023	29°Vi48'

1st House: my body, my identity, myself, my appearance, my projected image, my soul-purpose, initial approach to life, my interests, my sense of me
2nd House: my talents, my resources, my physical possessions, my money, my personal self-esteem, my sensuous enjoyment, my self-worth
3rd House: my adaptability, my communications, my siblings, my neighborhood, short journey, my active search for knowledge, learning, curiosity, thinking
4th House: my home, family, heritage, my privacy, my emotional life, feelings, eating habits, receptivity, my protective urges, vulnerability
5th House: my creative abilities, my self-expression pregnancy, children, pleasures, will power, romance, merry making, vacation, affection, confidence
6th House: my work conditions & habits, pets, my health, service offered, productivity, training, work skills, hygiene, clothing, nutrition & diet
7th House: agreements, contracts, partnerships, spouse, relationships, consultants, open enemies, receiving love, self-projection, social skills
8th House: loyalty, partner's money & resources, taxes, inheritance, psychic & occult, transformation, shared values, sexual energy, investigations
9th House: wisdom, justice, law, exploration, faith, religious & spiritual, higher education, foreign travel, legal action, experimentation, truth seeking
10th House: accomplishments, authority, recognition, success, reputation, professional affairs, maturity, proficiency, honor, self-fulfillment, public image/life
11th House: groups & clubs, trends, friends, political awareness, emotional detachment, progressive thought, innovative technology & inventions, astrology
12th House: concern for others, self-sacrifice, psychological health, escapism, drug use, pre-natal imprinting, secret keeping, surrender, spirituality

New

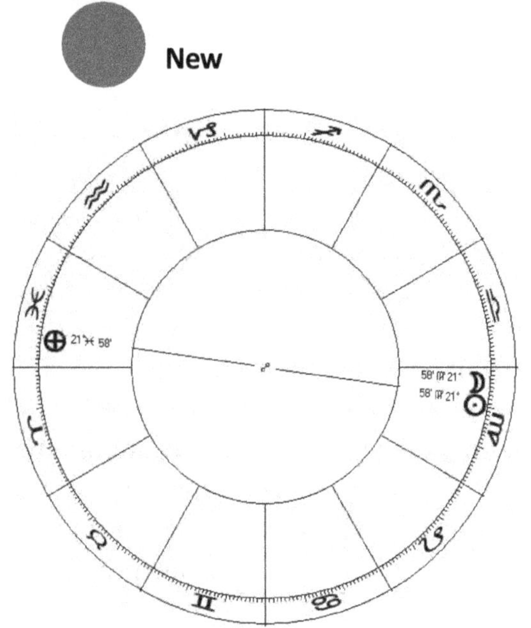

Sep 15 2023	1:39a	Moon 21°♍58'	Earth 21°♓58'	Sun 21°♍58'

What intuitive sense is emerging within me? Where do I sense my emotions in my body? Germination/Seedling/Germination
Moon & Sun in ♍ VIRGO: analytical, efficient, healing, health-conscious, exacting, technical
Earth in ♓ PISCES: spiritual, subtle, empathic, psychic, vulnerable, intuitive, self- sacrificing, artistic

I emerge with

Tarot, Spell, Oracle, Prayer for New Moon Phase:

Crescent

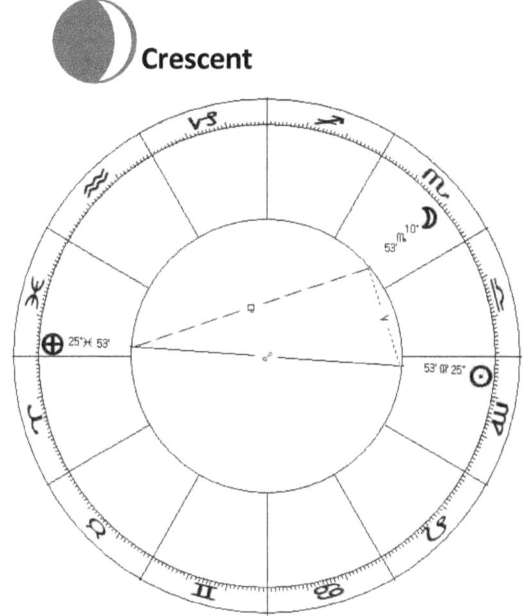

Sep 19 2023	2:00a	Moon 10°♏53'	Earth 25°♓53'	Sun 25°♍53'

What is my challenge? What is my promise? Is my ego an asset or a liability? Sprout
Moon in ♏ SCORPIO: transformative, sexual, secretive, musical, trust-worthy, loyal, supportive, jealous
Earth in ♓ PISCES: spiritual, subtle, empathic, psychic, vulnerable, intuitive, self- sacrificing, artistic
Sun in ♍ VIRGO: analytical, efficient, healing, health-conscious, exacting, technical

I challenge myself to

Tarot, Spell, Oracle, Prayer for Crescent Phase:

First Quarter

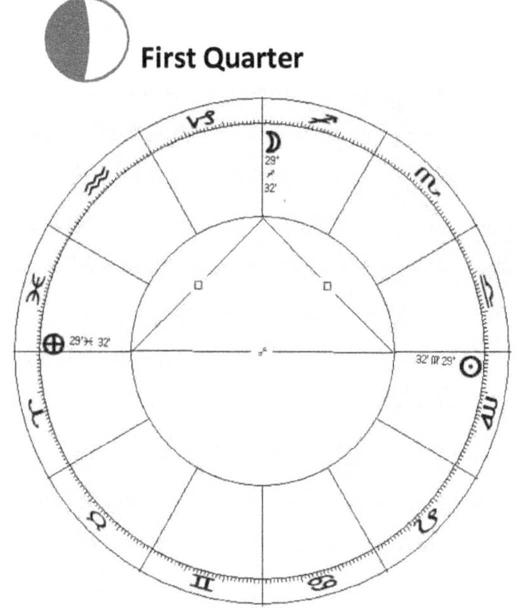

Sep 22 2023	7:31p	Moon 29°♐32'	Earth 29°♓32'	Sun 29°♍32'

What steps will I take toward accomplishing my goals? How do I move forward? Root/Stem/Leaf - photosynthesis
Moon in ♐ SAGITTARIUS: philosophical, truth-seeking, ethical, idealistic, optimistic, inspiring, wise, honest
Earth in ♓ PISCES: spiritual, subtle, empathic, psychic, vulnerable, intuitive, self- sacrificing, artistic
Sun in ♍ VIRGO: analytical, efficient, healing, health-conscious, exacting, technical

I take action on

Tarot, Spell, Oracle, Prayer for First Quarter Phase:

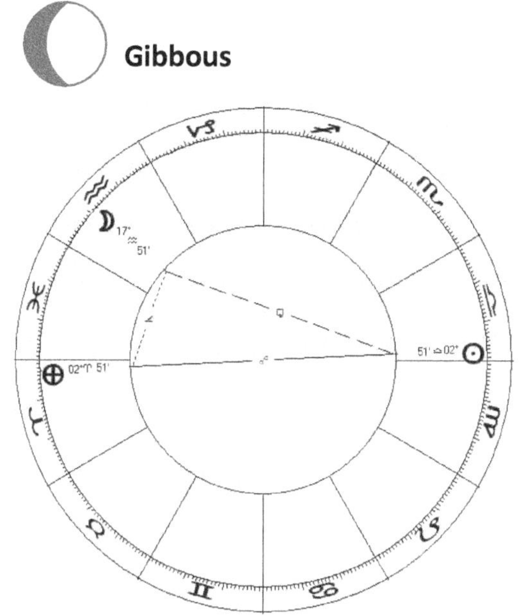

Sep 26 2023	4:44a	Moon 17°♒51'	Earth 02°♈51'	Sun 02°♎51'

How do I stay on track? What do I need to stay organized? What do I need to compromise? Buds appear and develop in size.
Moon in ♒ AQUARIUS: humanitarian, innovative, progressive, eccentric, detached, friendly
Earth in ♈ ARIES: assertive, courageous, athletic, independent, enthusiastic, aggressive, initiating
Sun in ♎ LIBRA: cooperative, fair, considerate, artistic, diplomatic, tactful, impartial, refined

I develop structure with

Tarot, Spell, Oracle, Prayer for Gibbous Phase:

Full

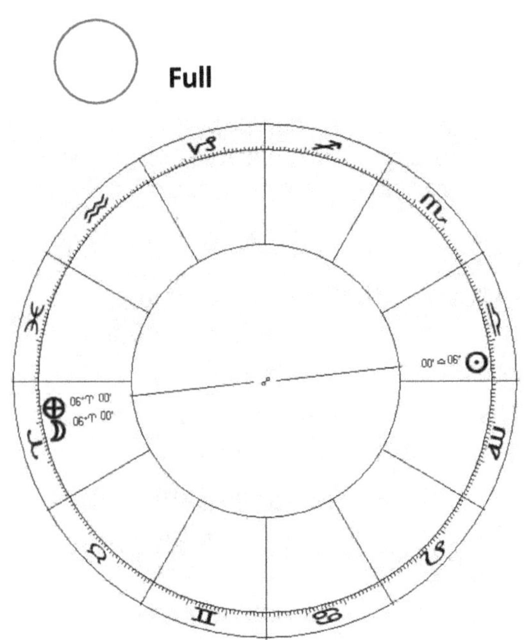

Sep 29 2023	9:57a	Moon 06°♈00'	Earth 06°♈00'	Sun 06°♎00'

How do function in my world with my process? What does it look like in my day-to-day world? Flower/Fruit

Moon & Earth in ♈ ARIES: assertive, courageous, independent, enthusiastic, aggressive, athletic, initiating

Sun in ♎ LIBRA: cooperative, fair, considerate, artistic, diplomatic, tactful, impartial, refined

I communicate my commitment to

Tarot, Spell, Oracle, Prayer for Full Moon Phase:

Disseminating

Oct 2 2023	6:59p	Moon 24° ♉ 19'	Earth 09° ♈ 19'	Sun 09° ♎ 19'

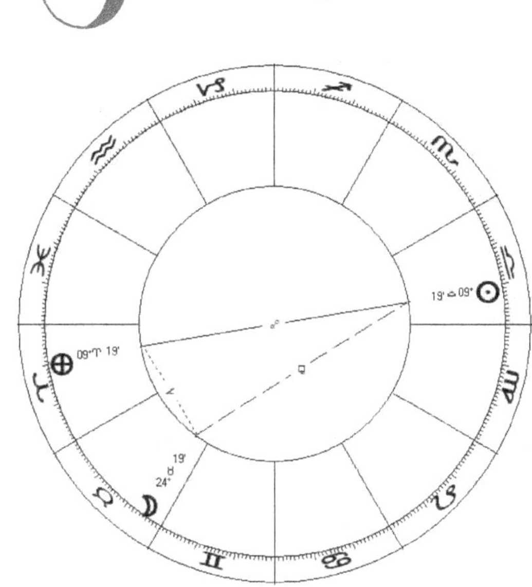

How can I share my experiences? How can I help others with my learning and experience? First harvest.
Moon in ♉ TAURUS: sensual, dependable, resourceful, deliberate, practical, comfortable, stubborn
Earth in ♈ ARIES: assertive, courageous, athletic, independent, enthusiastic, aggressive, initiating
Sun in ♎ LIBRA: cooperative, fair, considerate, artistic, diplomatic, tactful, impartial, refined

I share

Tarot, Spell, Oracle, Prayer for Disseminating Phase:

Last Quarter

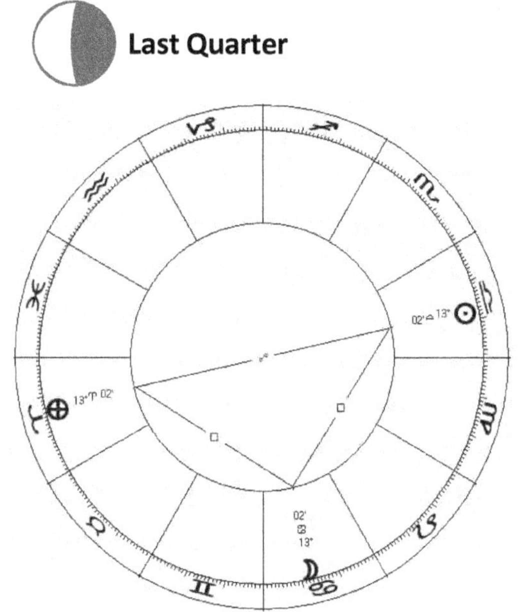

Oct 6 2023	1:47p	Moon 13°♋02'	Earth 13°♈02'	Sun 13°♎02'

How do I change- let go of the patterns that do not serve me and/or my community?
Decay/Last Harvest & composting.

Moon in ♋ CANCER: nurturing, attached, emotional, protective, psychic, domestic, intuitive

Earth in ♈ ARIES: assertive, courageous, athletic, independent, enthusiastic, aggressive, initiating

Sun in ♎ LIBRA: cooperative, fair, considerate, artistic, diplomatic, tactful, impartial, refined

I change perspective on

Tarot, Spell, Oracle, Prayer for Last Quarter Phase:

Balsamic

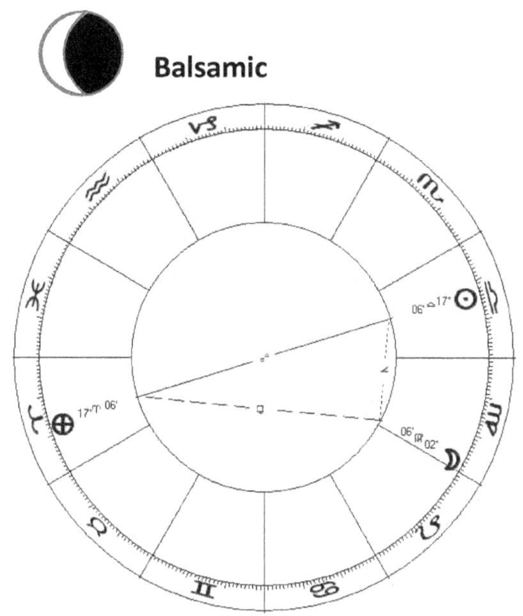

Oct 10 2023	4:16p	Moon 02°♍06'	Earth 17°♈06'	Sun 17°♎06'

How do I resolve this cycle & visualize, plan? Seed is planted, released to create next cycle/ germination begins.
Moon in ♍ VIRGO: analytical, efficient, healing health-conscious, exacting, technical
Earth in ♈ ARIES: assertive, courageous, athletic, independent, enthusiastic, aggressive, initiating
Sun in ♎ LIBRA: cooperative, fair, considerate, artistic, diplomatic, tactful, impartial, refined

I resolve/release and/or plan

Tarot, Spell, Oracle, Prayer for Balsamic Phase:

♎ Libra 2023

Ephemeris at Midnight UTC		
Oct 14 2023	11°Li57'	**1st House:** my body, my identity, myself, my appearance, my projected image, my soul-purpose, initial approach to life, my interests, my sense of me
Oct 15 2023	24°Li15'	
Oct 16 2023	06°Sc45'	**2nd House:** my talents, my resources, my physical possessions, my money, my personal self-esteem, my sensuous enjoyment, my self-worth
Oct 17 2023	19°Sc27'	
Oct 18 2023	02°Sg22'	**3rd House:** my adaptability, my communications, my siblings, my neighborhood, short journey, my active search for knowledge, learning, curiosity, thinking
Oct 19 2023	15°Sg32'	
Oct 20 2023	28°Sg55'	
Oct 21 2023	12°Cp33'	**4th House:** my home, family, heritage, my privacy, my emotional life, feelings, eating habits, receptivity, my protective urges, vulnerability
Oct 22 2023	26°Cp26'	
Oct 23 2023	10°Aq32'	
Oct 24 2023	24°Aq51'	**5th House:** my creative abilities, my self-expression pregnancy, children, pleasures, will power, romance, merry making, vacation, affection, confidence
Oct 25 2023	09°Pi20'	
Oct 26 2023	23°Pi54'	**6th House:** my work conditions & habits, pets, my health, service offered, productivity, training, work skills, hygiene, clothing, nutrition & diet
Oct 27 2023	08°Ar29'	
Oct 28 2023	22°Ar58'	
Oct 29 2023	07°Ta16'	**7th House:** agreements, contracts, partnerships, spouse, relationships, consultants, open enemies, receiving love, self-projection, social skills
Oct 30 2023	21°Ta19'	
Oct 31 2023	05°Ge01'	
Nov 1 2023	18°Ge21'	**8th House:** loyalty, partner's money & resources, taxes, inheritance, psychic & occult, transformation, shared values, sexual energy, investigations
Nov 2 2023	01°Cn19'	
Nov 3 2023	13°Cn57'	
Nov 4 2023	26°Cn16'	**9th House:** wisdom, justice, law, exploration, faith, religious & spiritual, higher education, foreign travel, legal action, experimentation, truth seeking
Nov 5 2023	08°Le21'	
Nov 6 2023	20°Le17'	**10th House:** accomplishments, authority, recognition, success, reputation, professional affairs, maturity, proficiency, honor, self-fulfillment, public image/life
Nov 7 2023	02°Vi08'	
Nov 8 2023	13°Vi59'	
Nov 9 2023	25°Vi55'	**11th House:** groups & clubs, trends, friends, political awareness, emotional detachment, progressive thought, innovative technology & inventions, astrology
Nov 10 2023	08°Li00'	
Nov 11 2023	20°Li17'	
Nov 12 2023	02°Sc48'	**12th House:** concern for others, self-sacrifice, psychological health, escapism, drug use, pre-natal imprinting, secret keeping, surrender, spirituality

New-Solar Annular Eclipse

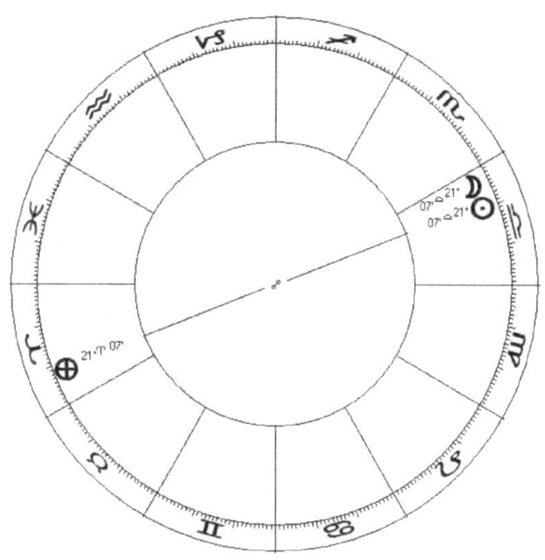

Oct 14 2023	5:55p	Moon 21°♎07'	Earth 21°♈07'	Sun 21°♎07'

What intuitive sense is emerging within me? Where do I sense my emotions in my body? Germination/Seedling/Germination
Moon & Sun in ♎ LIBRA: cooperative, fair, refined considerate, artistic, diplomatic, tactful, impartial,
Earth in ♈ ARIES: assertive, courageous, initiating, independent, athletic, enthusiastic, aggressive,

I emerge with

Tarot, Spell, Oracle, Prayer for New Moon Phase:

Crescent

Oct 18 2023	1:48p	Moon 09°♐55'	Earth 24°♈55'	Sun 24°♎55'

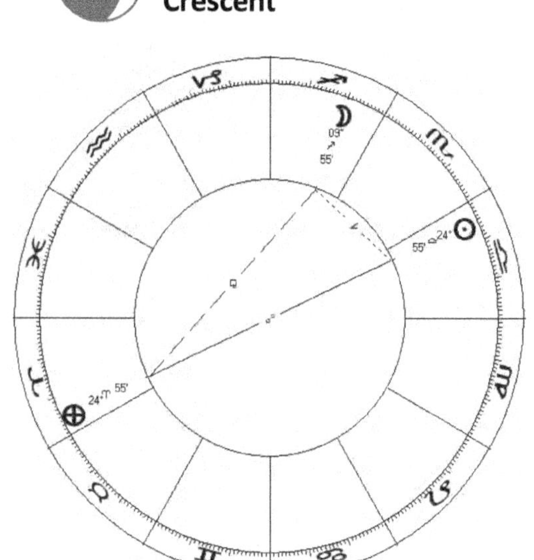

What is my challenge? What is my promise? Is my ego an asset or a liability? Sprout
Moon in ♐ SAGITTARIUS: philosophical, truth-seeking, ethical, idealistic, optimistic, inspiring, wise, honest
Earth in ♈ ARIES: assertive, courageous, athletic, independent, enthusiastic, aggressive, initiating
Sun in ♎ LIBRA: cooperative, fair, considerate, artistic, diplomatic, tactful, impartial, refined

I challenge myself to

Tarot, Spell, Oracle, Prayer for Crescent Phase:

First Quarter

Oct 22 2023	3:29a	Moon 28°♑28'	Earth 28°♈28'	Sun 28°♎28'

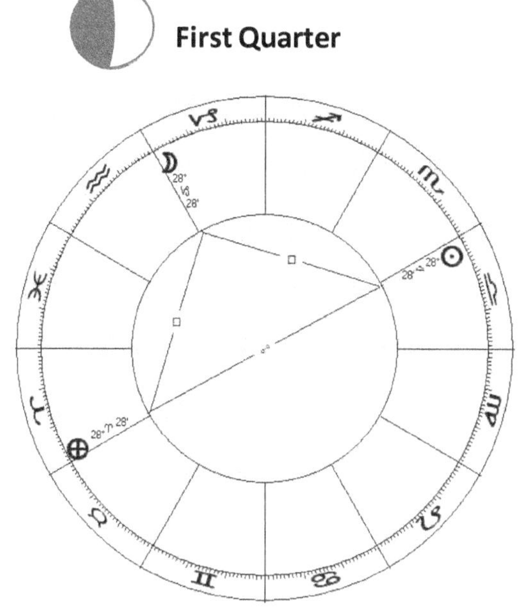

What steps will I take toward accomplishing my goals? How do I move forward? Root/Stem/Leaf - photosynthesis
Moon in ♑ CAPRICORN: disciplined, responsible, ambitious, professional, manifesting
Earth in ARIES: assertive, courageous, athletic, independent, enthusiastic, aggressive, initiating
Sun in ♎ LIBRA: cooperative, fair, considerate, artistic, diplomatic, tactful, impartial, refined

I take action on

Tarot, Spell, Oracle, Prayer for First Quarter Phase:

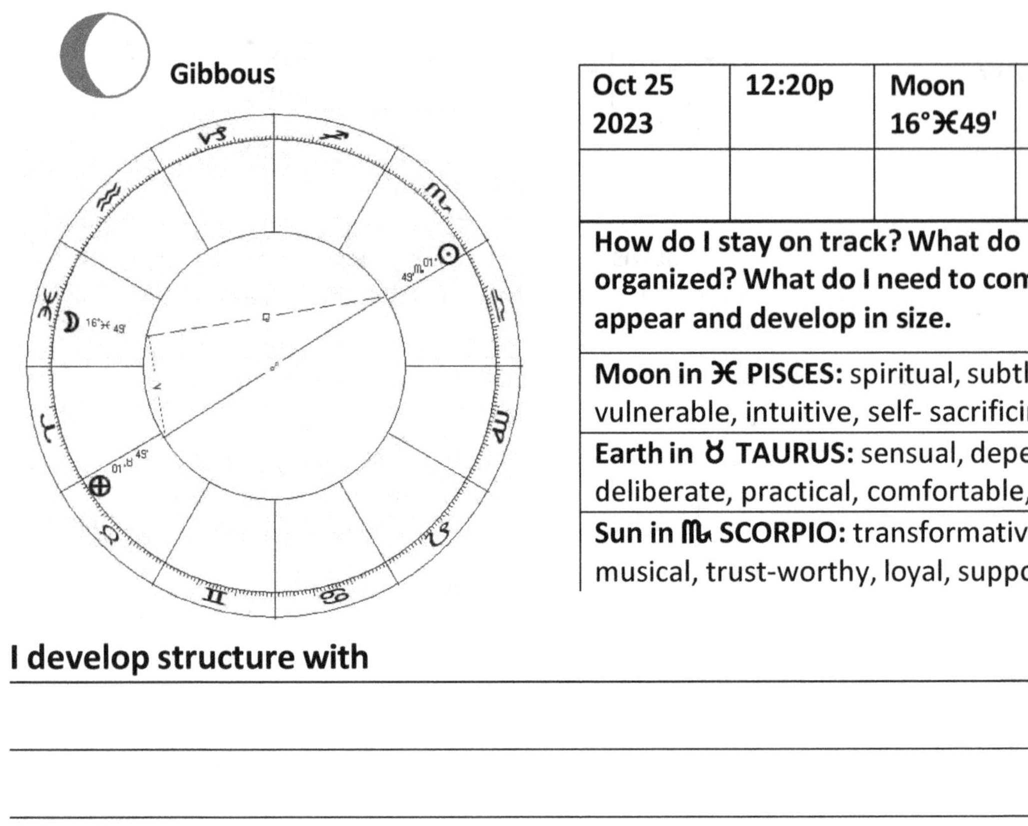

Gibbous

Oct 25 2023	12:20p	Moon 16°♓49'	Earth 01° ♉ 49'	Sun 01°♏49'
How do I stay on track? What do I need to stay organized? What do I need to compromise? Buds appear and develop in size.				
Moon in ♓ PISCES: spiritual, subtle, empathic, psychic, vulnerable, intuitive, self- sacrificing, artistic				
Earth in ♉ TAURUS: sensual, dependable, resourceful, deliberate, practical, comfortable, stubborn				
Sun in ♏ SCORPIO: transformative, sexual, secretive, musical, trust-worthy, loyal, supportive, jealous				

I develop structure with

Tarot, Spell, Oracle, Prayer for Gibbous Phase:

Full – Partial Lunar Eclipse

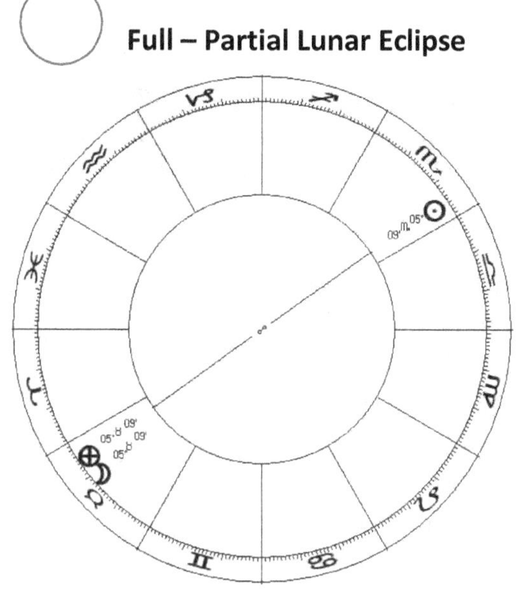

Oct 28 2023	8:24p	Moon 05° ♉ 09'	Earth 05° ♉ 09'	Sun 05°♏09'

How do function in my world with my process? What does it look like in my day-to-day world? Flower/Fruit
Moon & Earth in ♉ TAURUS: sensual, dependable, resourceful, deliberate, practical, comfortable, stubborn
Sun in ♏ SCORPIO: transformative, sexual, secretive, musical, trust-worthy, loyal, supportive, jealous

I communicate my commitment to

Tarot, Spell, Oracle, Prayer for Full Moon Phase:

Disseminating

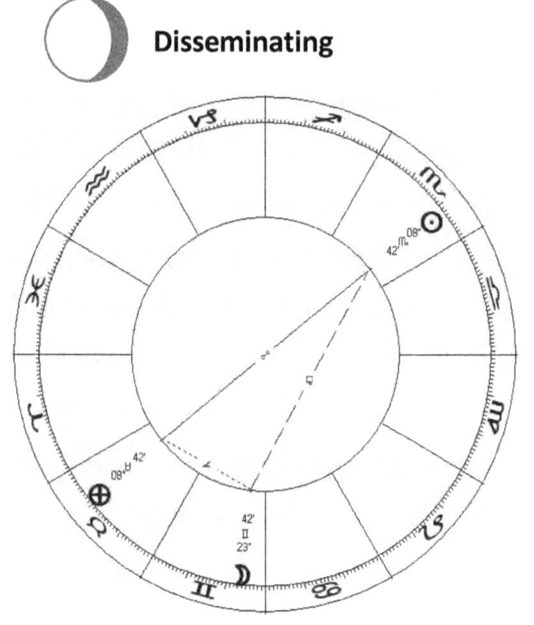

Nov 1 2023	9:48a	Moon 23° ♊ 42'	Earth 08° ♉ 42'	Sun 08° ♏ 42'

How can I share my experiences? How can I help others with my learning and experience? First harvest.
Moon in ♊ GEMINI: Clever, versatile, curious, articulate, adaptable, lighthearted, quick-witted, cheerful
Earth in ♉ TAURUS: sensual, dependable, resourceful, deliberate, practical, comfortable, stubborn
Sun in ♏ SCORPIO: transformative, sexual, secretive, musical, trust-worthy, loyal, supportive, jealous

I share

Tarot, Spell, Oracle, Prayer for Disseminating Phase:

Last Quarter

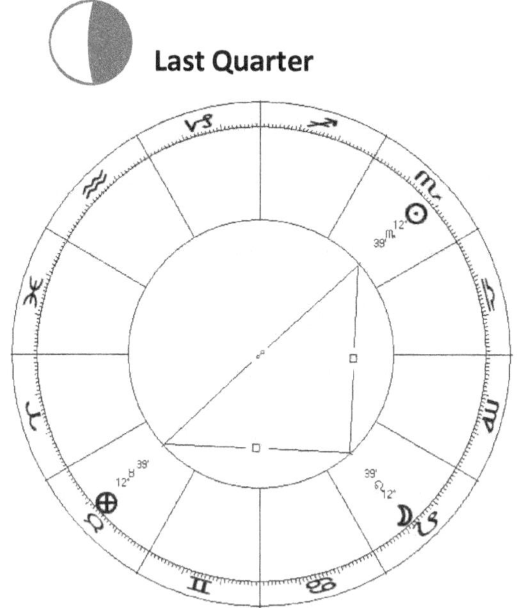

Nov 5 2023	8:36a	Moon 12°♌39'	Earth 12°♉39'	Sun 12°♏39'

How do I change- let go of the patterns that do not serve me and/or my community? Decay/Last Harvest & composting.
Moon in ♌ LEO: self-confident, generous, playful, dramatic, courageous, caring, brave, self-centered
Earth in ♉ TAURUS: sensual, dependable, resourceful, deliberate, practical, comfortable, stubborn
Sun in ♏ SCORPIO: transformative, sexual, secretive, musical, trust-worthy, loyal, supportive, jealous

I change perspective on

Tarot, Spell, Oracle, Prayer for Last Quarter Phase:

Balsamic

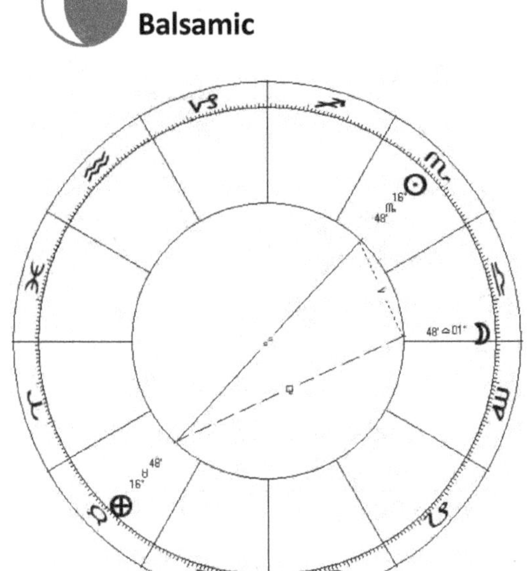

Nov 9 2023	11:43a	Moon 01°♎48'	Earth 16° ♉ 48'	Sun 16°♏48'

How do I resolve this cycle & visualize, plan? Seed is planted, released to create next cycle/ germination begins.
Moon in ♎ LIBRA: cooperative, fair, considerate, artistic, diplomatic, tactful, impartial, refined
Earth in ♉ TAURUS: sensual, dependable, resourceful, deliberate, practical, comfortable, stubborn
Sun in ♏ SCORPIO: transformative, sexual, secretive, musical, trust-worthy, loyal, supportive, jealous

I resolve/release and/or plan

Tarot, Spell, Oracle, Prayer for Balsamic Phase:

♏ Scorpio 2023

Ephemeris at Midnight UTC	
Nov 13 2023	15°Sc36'
Nov 14 2023	28°Sc41'
Nov 15 2023	12°Sg01'
Nov 16 2023	25°Sg36'
Nov 17 2023	09°Cp22'
Nov 18 2023	23°Cp18'
Nov 19 2023	07°Aq20'
Nov 20 2023	21°Aq27'
Nov 21 2023	05°Pi36'
Nov 22 2023	19°Pi46'
Nov 23 2023	03°Ar55'
Nov 24 2023	18°Ar02'
Nov 25 2023	02°Ta03'
Nov 26 2023	15°Ta55'
Nov 27 2023	29°Ta37'
Nov 28 2023	13°Ge04'
Nov 29 2023	26°Ge16'
Nov 30 2023	09°Cn09'
Dec 1 2023	21°Cn45'
Dec 2 2023	04°Le04'
Dec 3 2023	16°Le10'
Dec 4 2023	28°Le06'
Dec 5 2023	09°Vi56'
Dec 6 2023	21°Vi46'
Dec 7 2023	03°Li42'
Dec 8 2023	15°Li47'
Dec 9 2023	28°Li08'
Dec 10 2023	10°Sc47'
Dec 11 2023	23°Sc48'

1st House: my body, my identity, myself, my appearance, my projected image, my soul-purpose, initial approach to life, my interests, my sense of me
2nd House: my talents, my resources, my physical possessions, my money, my personal self-esteem, my sensuous enjoyment, my self-worth
3rd House: my adaptability, my communications, my siblings, my neighborhood, short journey, my active search for knowledge, learning, curiosity, thinking
4th House: my home, family, heritage, my privacy, my emotional life, feelings, eating habits, receptivity, my protective urges, vulnerability
5th House: my creative abilities, my self-expression pregnancy, children, pleasures, will power, romance, merry making, vacation, affection, confidence
6th House: my work conditions & habits, pets, my health, service offered, productivity, training, work skills, hygiene, clothing, nutrition & diet
7th House: agreements, contracts, partnerships, spouse, relationships, consultants, open enemies, receiving love, self-projection, social skills
8th House: loyalty, partner's money & resources, taxes, inheritance, psychic & occult, transformation, shared values, sexual energy, investigations
9th House: wisdom, justice, law, exploration, faith, religious & spiritual, higher education, foreign travel, legal action, experimentation, truth seeking
10th House: accomplishments, authority, recognition, success, reputation, professional affairs, maturity, proficiency, honor, self-fulfillment, public image/life
11th House: groups & clubs, trends, friends, political awareness, emotional detachment, progressive thought, innovative technology & inventions, astrology
12th House: concern for others, self-sacrifice, psychological health, escapism, drug use, pre-natal imprinting, secret keeping, surrender, spirituality

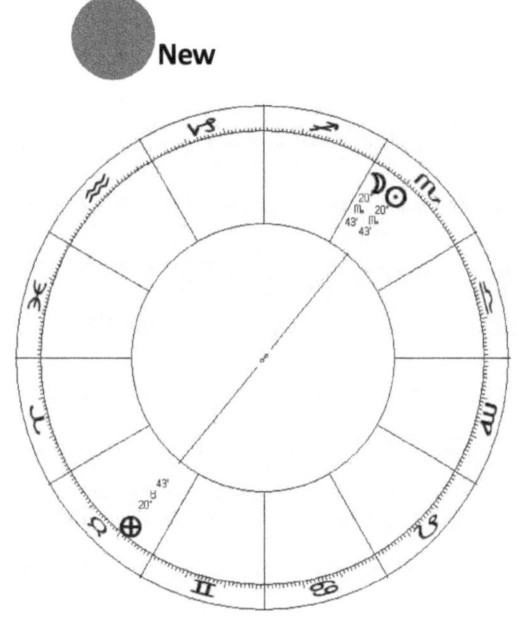

Nov 13 2023	9:27a	Moon 20°♏43'	Earth 20° ♉ 43'	Sun 20°♏43'

What intuitive sense is emerging within me? Where do I sense my emotions in my body? Germination/Seedling/Germination
Moon & Sun in ♏ SCORPIO: transformative, sexual, secretive, musical, trust-worthy, loyal, supportive, jealous
Earth in ♉ TAURUS: sensual, dependable, resourceful, deliberate, practical, comfortable, stubborn

I emerge with

Tarot, Spell, Oracle, Prayer for New Moon Phase:

Crescent

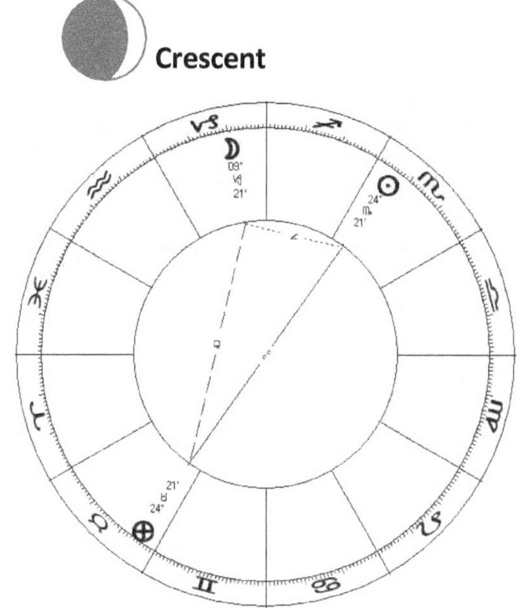

Nov 16 2023	11:58p	Moon 09°♑21'	Earth 24°♉21'	Sun 24°♏21'

What is my challenge? What is my promise? Is my ego an asset or liability? Sprout
Moon in ♑ CAPRICORN: disciplined, responsible, ambitious, professional, manifesting
Earth in ♉ TAURUS: sensual, dependable, resourceful, deliberate, practical, comfortable, stubborn
Sun in ♏ SCORPIO: transformative, sexual, secretive, musical, trustworthy loyal, supportive, jealous

I challenge myself to

Tarot, Spell, Oracle, Prayer for Crescent Phase:

First Quarter

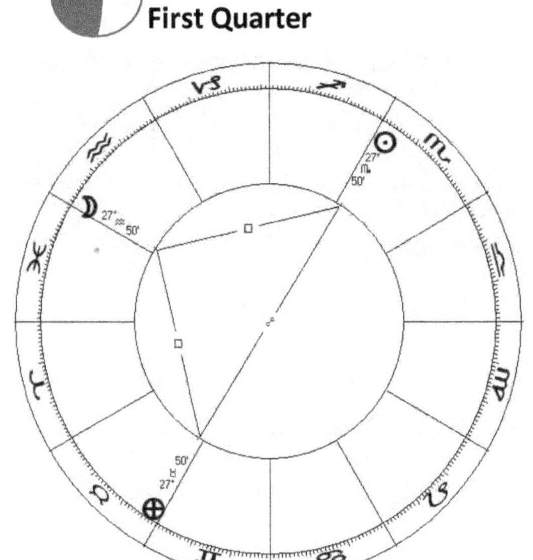

Nov 20 2023	10:49a	Moon 27°♒50'	Earth 27°♉50'	Sun 27°♏50'

What steps will I take toward accomplishing my goals? How do I move forward? Root/Stem/Leaf - photosynthesis
Moon in ♒ AQUARIUS: humanitarian, innovative, progressive, eccentric, detached, friendly
Earth in ♉ TAURUS: sensual, dependable, resourceful, deliberate, practical, comfortable, stubborn
Sun in ♏ SCORPIO: transformative, sexual, secretive, musical, trustworthy, loyal, supportive, jealous

I take action on

Tarot, Spell, Oracle, Prayer for First Quarter Phase:

Gibbous

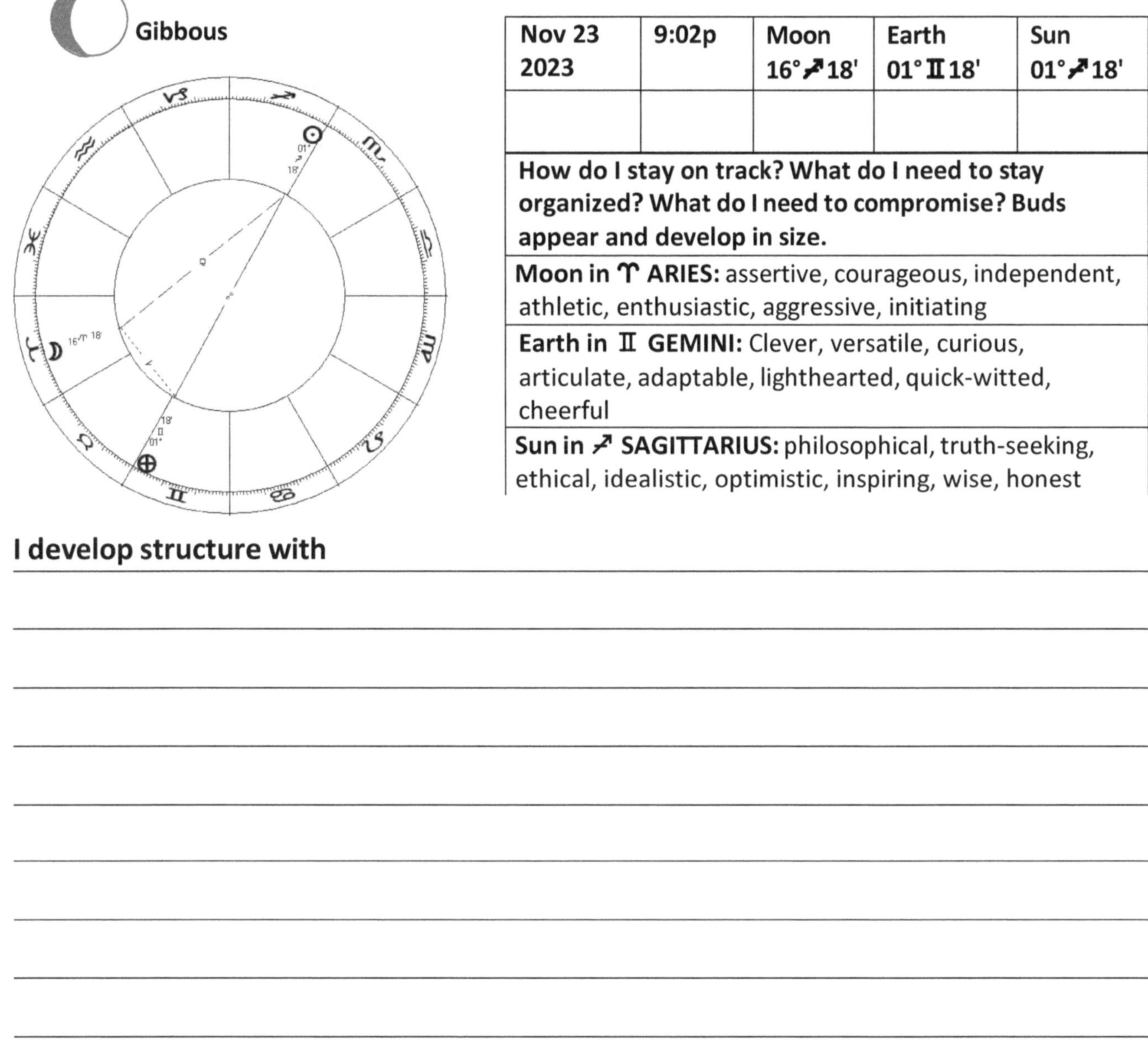

Nov 23 2023	9:02p	Moon 16°♐18'	Earth 01°♊18'	Sun 01°♐18'

How do I stay on track? What do I need to stay organized? What do I need to compromise? Buds appear and develop in size.
Moon in ♈ ARIES: assertive, courageous, independent, athletic, enthusiastic, aggressive, initiating
Earth in ♊ GEMINI: Clever, versatile, curious, articulate, adaptable, lighthearted, quick-witted, cheerful
Sun in ♐ SAGITTARIUS: philosophical, truth-seeking, ethical, idealistic, optimistic, inspiring, wise, honest

I develop structure with

Tarot, Spell, Oracle, Prayer for Gibbous Phase:

Full

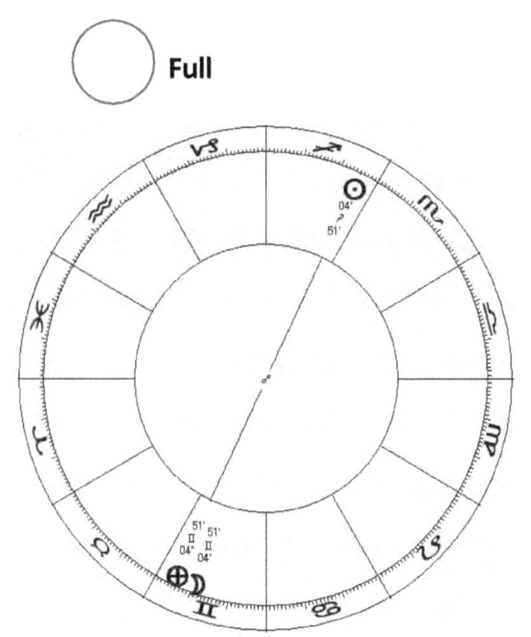

Nov 27 2023	9:16a	Moon 04° ♊ 51'	Earth 04 ♊ °51'	Sun 04° ♐ 51'

How do function in my world with my process? What does it look like in my day-to-day world? Flower/Fruit
Moon in & Earth in ♊ GEMINI: Clever, versatile, curious, articulate, adaptable, lighthearted, quick-witted, cheerful
Sun in ♐ SAGITTARIUS: philosophical, truth-seeking, ethical, idealistic, optimistic, inspiring, wise, honest

I communicate my commitment to

Tarot, Spell, Oracle, Prayer for Full Moon Phase:

Disseminating

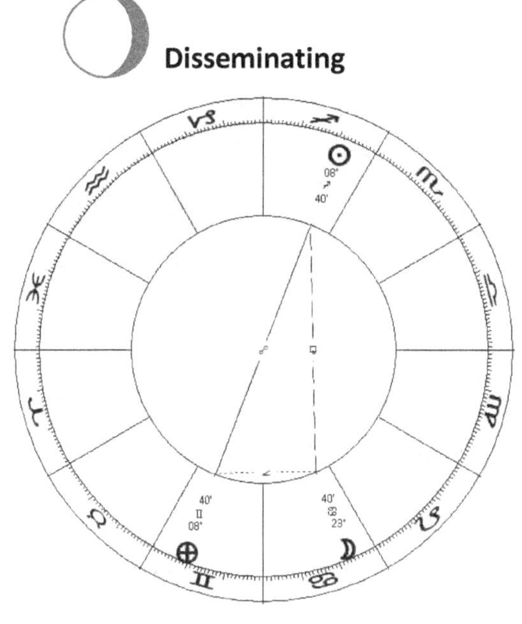

Dec 1 2023	3:41a	Moon 23°♋40'	Earth 08°♊40'	Sun 08°♐40'

How can I share my experiences? How can I help others with my learning and experience? First harvest.
Moon in ♋ CANCER: nurturing, attached, emotional, protective, psychic, domestic, intuitive
Earth in ♊ GEMINI: Clever, versatile, curious, articulate, adaptable, lighthearted, quick-witted, cheerful
Sun in ♐ SAGITTARIUS: philosophical, truth-seeking, ethical, idealistic, optimistic, inspiring, wise, honest

I share

Tarot, Spell, Oracle, Prayer for Disseminating Phase:

Last Quarter

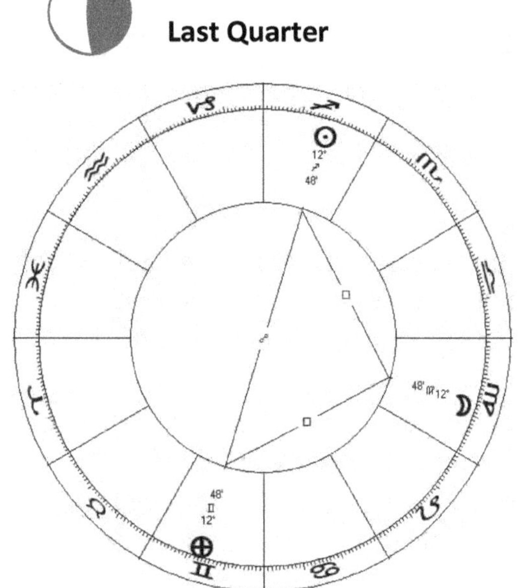

Dec 5 2023	5:49a	Moon 12°♍48'	Earth 12°♊48'	Sun 12°♐48'

How do I change- let go of the patterns that do not serve me and/or my community? Decay/Last Harvest & composting.
Moon in ♍ VIRGO: analytical, efficient, healing health-conscious, exacting, technical
Earth in ♊ GEMINI: Clever, versatile, curious, articulate, adaptable, lighthearted, quick-witted, cheerful
Sun in ♐ SAGITTARIUS: philosophical, truth-seeking, ethical, idealistic, optimistic, inspiring, wise, honest

I change perspective on

Tarot, Spell, Oracle, Prayer for Last Quarter Phase:

Balsamic

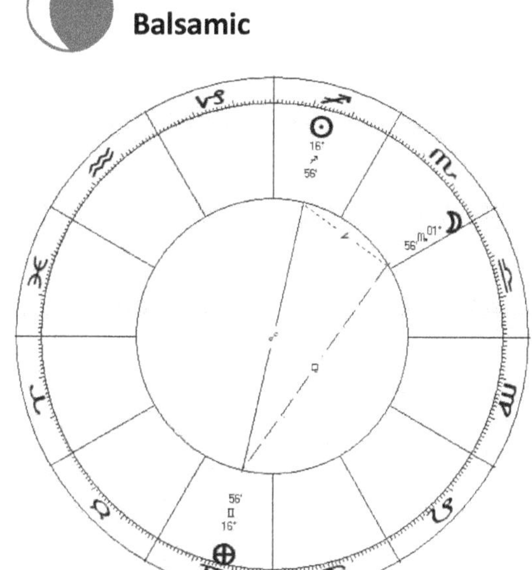

Dec 9 2023	7:16a	Moon 01°♏56'	Earth 16°♊56'	Sun 16°♐56'

How do I resolve this cycle & visualize, plan? Seed is planted, released to create next cycle/ germination begins.
Moon in ♏ SCORPIO: transformative, sexual, secretive, musical, trust-worthy, loyal, supportive, jealous
Earth in ♊ GEMINI: Clever, versatile, curious, articulate, adaptable, lighthearted, quick-witted, cheerful
Sun in ♐ SAGITTARIUS: philosophical, truth-seeking, ethical, idealistic, optimistic, inspiring, wise, honest

I resolve/release and/or plan

Tarot, Spell, Oracle, Prayer for Balsamic Phase:

♐ Sagittarius 2023

Ephemeris at Midnight UTC		
Dec 12 2023	07°Sg11'	**1st House:** my body, my identity, myself, my appearance, my projected image, my soul-purpose, initial approach to life, my interests, my sense of me
Dec 13 2023	20°Sg56'	
Dec 14 2023	04°Cp59'	**2nd House:** my talents, my resources, my physical possessions, my money, my personal self-esteem, my sensuous enjoyment, my self-worth
Dec 15 2023	19°Cp15'	
Dec 16 2023	03°Aq38'	**3rd House:** my adaptability, my communications, my siblings, my neighborhood, short journey, my active search for knowledge, learning, curiosity, thinking
Dec 17 2023	18°Aq03'	
Dec 18 2023	02°Pi24'	
Dec 19 2023	16°Pi37'	**4th House:** my home, family, heritage, my privacy, my emotional life, feelings, eating habits, receptivity, my protective urges, vulnerability
Dec 20 2023	00°Ar42'	
Dec 21 2023	14°Ar37'	
Dec 22 2023	28°Ar23'	**5th House:** my creative abilities, my self-expression pregnancy, children, pleasures, will power, romance, merry making, vacation, affection, confidence
Dec 23 2023	11°Ta58'	
Dec 24 2023	25°Ta25'	**6th House:** my work conditions & habits, pets, my health, service offered, productivity, training, work skills, hygiene, clothing, nutrition & diet
Dec 25 2023	08°Ge41'	
Dec 26 2023	21°Ge47'	
Dec 27 2023	04°Cn40'	**7th House:** agreements, contracts, partnerships, spouse, relationships, consultants, open enemies, receiving love, self-projection, social skills
Dec 28 2023	17°Cn20'	
Dec 29 2023	29°Cn48'	
Dec 30 2023	12°Le02'	**8th House:** loyalty, partner's money & resources, taxes, inheritance, psychic & occult, transformation, shared values, sexual energy, investigations
Dec 31 2023	24°Le05'	
Jan 1 2024	05°Vi59'	
Jan 2 2024	"17°Vi48'"	**9th House:** wisdom, justice, law, exploration, faith, religious & spiritual, higher education, foreign travel, legal action, experimentation, truth seeking
Jan 3 2024	"29°Vi36'"	
Jan 4 2024	"11°Li29'"	
Jan 5 2024	"23°Li32'"	**10th House:** accomplishments, authority, recognition, success, reputation, professional affairs, maturity, proficiency, honor, self-fulfillment, public image/life
Jan 6 2024	"05°Sc51'"	
Jan 7 2024	"18°Sc30'"	
Jan 8 2024	"01°Sg34'"	**11th House:** groups & clubs, trends, friends, political awareness, emotional detachment, progressive thought, innovative technology & inventions, astrology
Jan 9 2024	"15°Sg06'"	
Jan 10 2024	"29°Sg04'"	
Jan 11 2024	"13°Cp27'"	**12th House:** concern for others, self-sacrifice, psychological health, escapism, drug use, pre-natal imprinting, secret keeping, surrender, spirituality

New

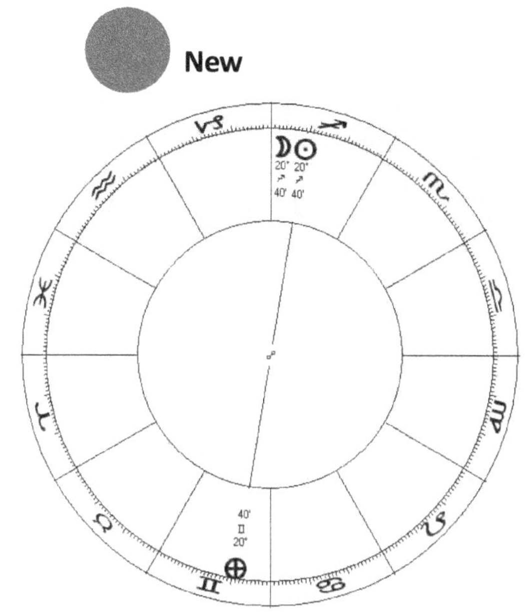

Dec 12 2023	11:32p	Moon 20°♐40'	Earth 20°♊40'	Sun 20°♐40'

What intuitive sense is emerging within me? Where do I sense my emotions in my body? Germination/Seedling/Germination

Moon & Sun in ♐ SAGITTARIUS: philosophical, truth-seeking, ethical, idealistic, optimistic, inspiring, wise, honest

Earth in , GEMINI: Clever, versatile, curious, articulate, adaptable, lighthearted, quick-witted, cheerful

I emerge with

Tarot, Spell, Oracle, Prayer for New Moon Phase:

Crescent

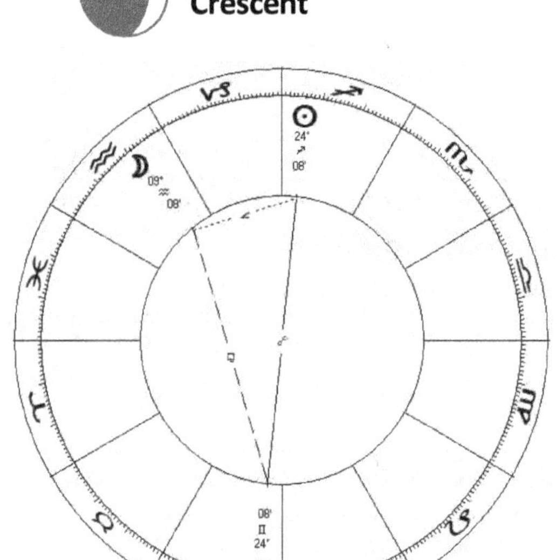

Dec 16 2023	9:08a	Moon 09°♒08'	Earth 24° ♊ 08'	Sun 24° ♐ 08'

What is my challenge? What is my promise? Is my ego an asset or liability? Sprout
Moon in ♒ AQUARIUS: humanitarian, innovative, progressive, eccentric, detached, friendly
Earth in ♊ GEMINI: Clever, versatile, curious, articulate, adaptable, lighthearted, quick-witted, cheerful
Sun in ♐ SAGITTARIUS: philosophical, truth-seeking, ethical, idealistic, optimistic, inspiring, wise, honest

I challenge myself to

Tarot, Spell, Oracle, Prayer for Crescent Phase:

First Quarter

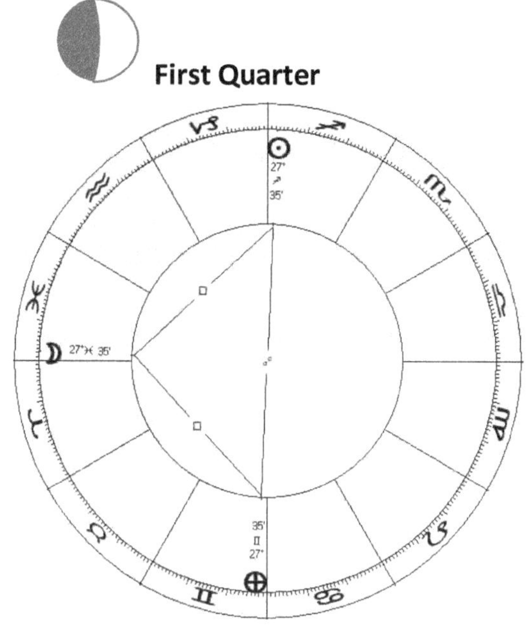

Dec 19 2023	6:39p	Moon 27°♓35'	Earth 27°♊35'	Sun 27°♐35'

What steps will I take toward accomplishing my goals? How do I move forward? Root/Stem/Leaf - photosynthesis

Moon in ♓ PISCES: spiritual, subtle, empathic, psychic, vulnerable, intuitive, self- sacrificing, artistic

Earth in ♊ GEMINI: Clever, versatile, curious, articulate, adaptable, lighthearted, quick-witted, cheerful

Sun in ♐ SAGITTARIUS: philosophical, truth-seeking, ethical, idealistic, optimistic, inspiring, wise, honest

I take action on

Tarot, Spell, Oracle, Prayer for First Quarter Phase:

Gibbous

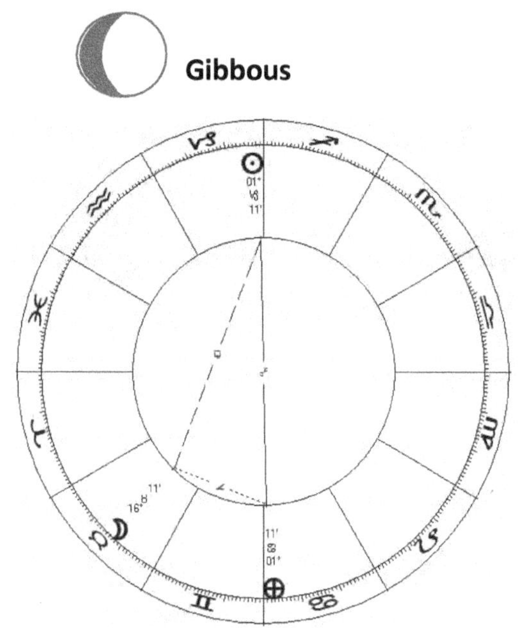

Dec 23 2023	7:28a	Moon 16° ♉ 11'	Earth 01° ♋ 11'	Sun 01° ♑ 11'

How do I stay on track? What do I need to stay organized? What do I need to compromise? Buds appear and develop in size.
Moon in ♉ TAURUS: sensual, dependable, resourceful, deliberate, practical, comfortable, stubborn
Earth in ♋ CANCER: nurturing, attached, emotional, protective, psychic, domestic, intuitive
Sun in ♑ CAPRICORN: disciplined, responsible, ambitious, professional, manifesting

I develop structure with

Tarot, Spell, Oracle, Prayer for Gibbous Phase:

Full

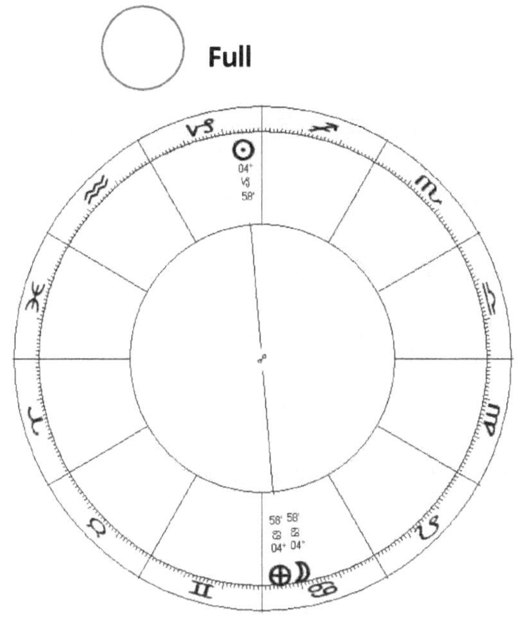

Dec 27 2023	0:33a	Moon 04°♋58'	Earth 04°♋58'	Sun 04°♑58'

How do function in my world with my process? What does it look like in my day-to-day world? Flower/Fruit
Moon & Earth in ♋ CANCER: nurturing, attached, emotional, protective, psychic, domestic, intuitive
Sun in ♑CAPRICORN: disciplined, responsible, ambitious, professional, manifesting

I communicate my commitment to

Tarot, Spell, Oracle, Prayer for Full Moon Phase:

Disseminating

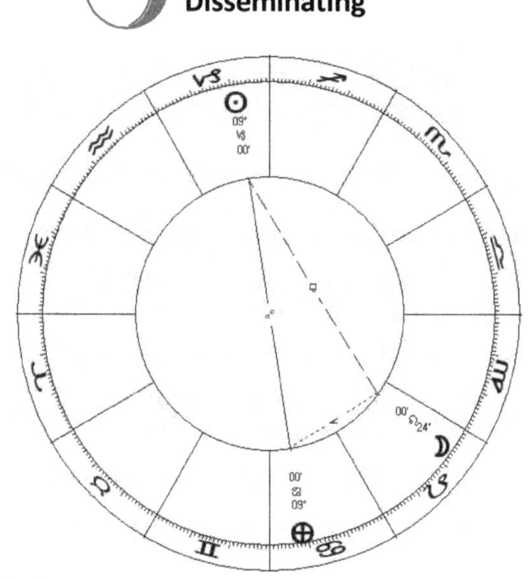

Dec 30 2023	11:50p	Moon 24°♌00'	Earth 09°♋00'	Sun 09°♑00'

How can I share my experiences? How can I help others with my learning and experience? First harvest.
Moon in ♌ LEO: self-confident, generous, playful, dramatic, courageous, caring, brave, self-centered
Earth in ♋ CANCER: nurturing, attached, emotional, protective, psychic, domestic, intuitive
Sun in ♑CAPRICORN: disciplined, responsible, ambitious, professional, manifesting

I share

Tarot, Spell, Oracle, Prayer for Disseminating Phase:

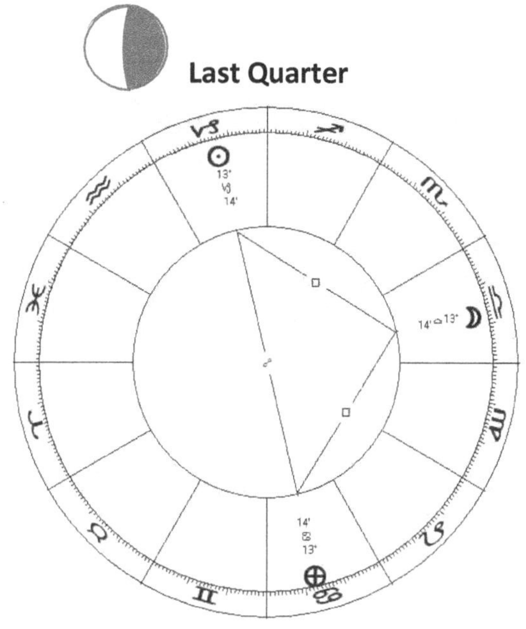

Jan 4 2024	3:30a	Moon 13°♎14'	Earth 13°♋14'	Sun 13°♑14'

How do I change- let go of the patterns that do not serve me and/or my community? Decay/Last Harvest & composting.
Moon in ♎ LIBRA: cooperative, fair, considerate, artistic, diplomatic, tactful, impartial, refined
Earth in ♋ CANCER: nurturing, attached, emotional, protective, psychic, domestic, intuitive
Sun in ♑ CAPRICORN: disciplined, responsible, ambitious, professional, manifesting

I change perspective on

Tarot, Spell, Oracle, Prayer for Last QuarterPhase:

Balsamic

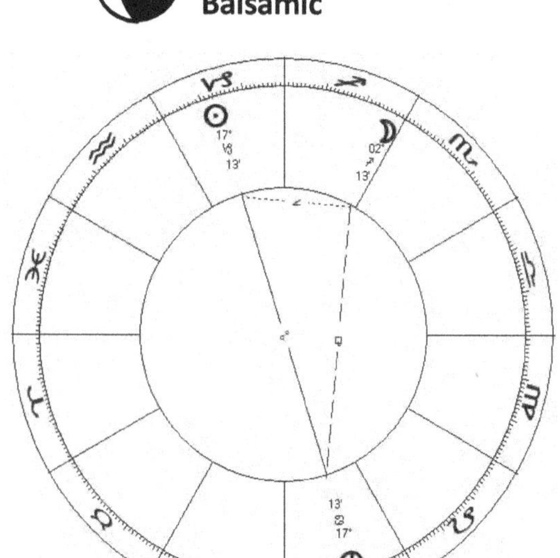

Jan 8 2024	1:09a	Moon 02°♐13'	Earth 17°♋13'	Sun 17°♑13'

How do I resolve this cycle & visualize, plan? Seed is planted, released to create next cycle/ germination begins.
Moon in ♐ SAGITTARIUS: philosophical, truth-seeking, ethical, idealistic, optimistic, inspiring, wise, honest
Earth in ♋ CANCER: nurturing, attached, emotional, protective, psychic, domestic, intuitive
Sun in ♑ CAPRICORN: disciplined, responsible, ambitious, professional**,** manifesting

I resolve/release and/or plan

Tarot, Spell, Oracle, Prayer for Balsamic Phase:

Time Zone Conversion

- The Green Mountain Moon Journal is created inCoordinated Universal Time (UTC or UT), using the Tropical Zodiac.
- Please note that no matter which time zone you live in, the zodiac degrees of the moon's phase are the same.
- When you know the plus+ or minus - from UTC of your own time zone is, each phase time can be easily adjusted; further adjustment may be needed if Daylight Savings or other seasonal time changes are used in your time zone. UTC does not use Daylight Savings Time but stays constant. It is the same as GMT (Greenwich Mean Time).

Here are some online links for Time Zone Conversion and Moon Phase

Calculation: TIME ZONE LIST: https://www.timeanddate.com/time/zones/

INTERACTIVE CALCULATOR: https://www.timeanddate.com/time/map/

www.ingramcontent.com/pod-product-compliance
Lightning Source LLC
Chambersburg PA
CBHW081848110426
42740CB00066B/3200

* 9 7 9 8 2 1 8 1 0 7 2 0 8 *